D1573860

DOLOMITEN

DOLOMITEN

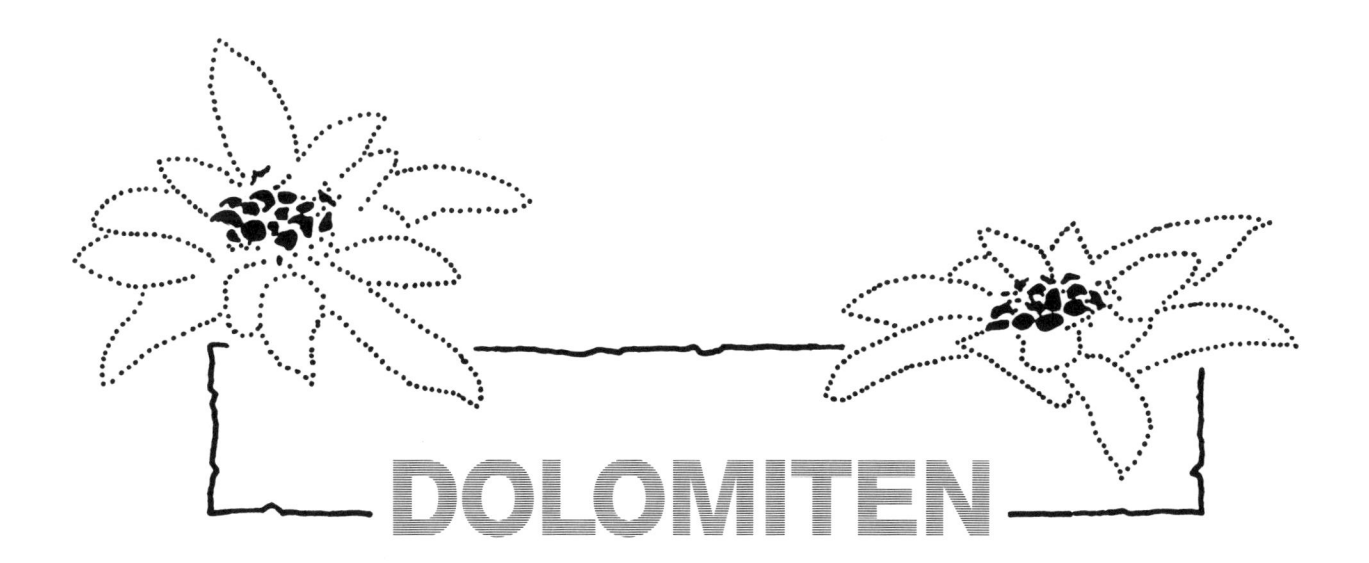

DOLOMITES

Unveränderte Neuauflage 1999
Alle Rechte der deutschen Ausgabe
© 1992, 1999 J. Berg bei Bruckmann
ISBN 3-7654-3452-3

© 1991, Priuli & Verlucca, editori
C.P. 245 / 10015 Ivrea (Italy)

Alle Rechte vorbehalten

Printed in Italy

Druck: Musumeci, Aoste

Lithografie: Garbero, Turin

Übersetzung ins Englische: John Iliffe
Übersetzung ins Deutsche: Gabriele Karg
Gestaltung des Schutzumschlags: Wolfgang Lauter, München

Bildnachweis: Alle Fotos, mit Ausnahme folgender Bildnummern,
stammen von A. Boccazzi-Varotto:
A. Bernard, Predazzo, Bild-Nr. 17 u. 54, L. Eccher, Trient, Bild-Nr. 35 u. 42,
B. Flaim, Bozen, Bild-Nr. 46 u. 51.

DOLOMITEN
360°

FOTOGRAFIE / PHOTOGRAPHS:
ATTILIO BOCCAZZI-VAROTTO

TEXT:
ROBERTO FESTI

VERLAG J. BERG BEI BRUCKMANN

Text
Roberto Festi

Vor noch nicht allzu langer Zeit führte ich ein einzigartiges Experiment durch: Ich fragte eine ziemlich große Anzahl von Personen, ob sie die Dolomiten kennen. Die Frage wurde stets mit »ja« beantwortet. Unter den vielen Befragten — gleich welcher Nation — zögerte nicht einer mit der Antwort.

Auf die weitere Frage, wo sich diese berühmte Gebirgsgruppe denn befinde, kamen erste Unsicherheiten auf; die wenigsten konnten die genaue geographische Lage oder die Provinzen angeben, einige versuchten ziemlich vage, das Gebiet mit bekannteren Orten und Gegenden in Verbindung zu bringen: »... next to Venice..., in der Nähe des Gardasees..., in Südtirol..., zwischen Bozen und Österreich...«

Das Experiment ist gelungen! Und das Ergebnis eindeutig: Der internationalen Berühmtheit der Dolomiten steht jede Menge Unsicherheit über ihre genaue geographische Lage gegenüber. Das ist kein Vorwurf an die befragten Personen, aber die Antworten sind bezeichnend und beweisen, daß Berühmtheit nicht unbedingt mit genauer Information Hand in Hand geht.

Diese Unsicherheit wurde in den vergangenen Jahren durch eine Fülle von Veröffentlichungen verschlimmert. Obwohl diese Bücher, die sich vorwiegend an Wanderer und naturkundlich oder geologisch interessierte Leser wandten, umfassend waren und immer wieder auf den neuesten Stand gebracht wurden, basierten sie oft auf falschen geographischen Zuordnungen zu einzelnen Provinzen; sie vergaßen nämlich die Tatsache, daß die Berge, wie andere natürlich begrenzte Gebiete, ein gemeinsames Erbe ausbilden, unabhängig von politischen Grenzen.

200 Jahre nachdem die Berge unter dem Namen »Dolomiten« ins Reich der Wissenschaft aufgenommen worden sind, versuchten die Bewohner ihrer Talschaften im Geiste ihres gemeinsamen naturgegebenen Vaterlandes auf verschiedene Art und Weise, den Schwerpunkt dieser zweihundertjährigen Geschichte richtig zu setzen; 200 Jahre, die vor allem auch an das Erwachen eines neuen Forschergeistes im Europa zur Zeit der Aufklärung erinnern.

Auch die heutige Berühmtheit der Dolomiten hängt eng mit ihrer Entdeckung zusammen. Es war im Jahre 1788, als der französische Geologe Déodat Tancred de Dolomieu zum ersten Mal die außergewöhnlichen Charaktereigenschaften des dolomitischen Gesteins bestimmte. In der Tat kann die Reise Dolomieus durch dieses Gebirge, das ihm so »einzigartig und unwirklich« erschien, als der Beginn seines neuzeitlichen Schicksals gelten; eines Schicksals, das von nun an von einem stetig wachsenden Interesse an den natürlichen Schönheiten dieser Region bestimmt wurde, die bald schon als die Ideallandschaft für Wanderer und Bergsteiger galt.

Und tatsächlich ist es die geologische Beschaffenheit, die die Dolomiten begrenzt. Diese Kette der Alpen, die gewöhnlich in einen östlichen und einen westlichen Teil untergliedert wird, liegt in den Provinzen Belluno, Bozen und Trento und wird vom Verlauf der Flüsse Eisack,

Etsch, Piave, Rienz, Cismon und Brenta begrenzt. Zu den Dolomiten werden auch die ausgedehnte Brentagruppe gezählt, im Trentino, zwischen den Flüssen Etsch, Sarca und Noce gelegen, sowie die kleinen Dolomiten, die die Lessini- und Pasubiogruppe in der Voralpenregion des Veneto miteinander verbindet.

Die wissenschaftliche Entdeckung Dolomieus markiert gleichsam die neuzeitliche Geburt dieser wunderbaren Felskolosse, die wirklich lebendig zu sein scheinen — rot in der Abenddämmerung, wenn die letzten Sonnenstrahlen die rauhen Zinnen umzüngeln, weiß wie der Mond in den Nachtstunden, was ihnen den Namen »Bleiche Berge« eingetragen hat. Ihre eigentliche Entstehung liegt aber gut 250 Millionen Jahre zurück. Damals entstand durch eruptive Vorgänge ein Meer, das von unzähligen Kolonien verschiedener Organismen bevölkert wurde. Diese Kleinstlebewesen schufen, Schicht für Schicht, enorme Korallenriffs. Nach dem Rückzug des Wassers wurden sie durch die eiszeitliche Formung immer deutlicher herausmodelliert.

Doch diese komplexen geologischen Vorgänge, die zum Teil noch heute andauern, sollen hier nicht weiter dargelegt werden. Es genügt, an dieser Stelle Dolomieus ersten wissenschaftlichen Befund über dieses Gestein anzuführen, der die Grundlage zahlreicher weiterer Untersuchungen der Dolomiten bildete: »...es handelt sich um einen schwach efferverzierenden Kalkstein, der die Granitberge zwischen Trient und Bozen umgibt und in vielen Fällen bedeckt.«

Die Entdeckung des französischen Wissenschaftlers regte zu Beginn des 19. Jahrhunderts zu zahlreichen weiteren Studienreisen an. Zu dieser Zeit — die Geheimnisse des Montblancs und der übrigen Westalpen waren bereits gelüftet — wuchs das Interesse an den Dolomiten. Neue Erkenntnisse wurden gewonnen, diese regten weitere Besucher an, und so bildete sich allmählich jener »Mythos«, der auch heute noch diese faszinierende Hochgebirgslandschaft umgibt.

Geschichte und Legende sind in dieser Bergwelt eng miteinander verknüpft. Es ist eine Welt voller Aberglauben, voller göttlicher und phantastischer Wesen. Dieser Aberglaube war die Quelle einer ehrfuchtsvollen Angst vor den Bergen, die aus diesem Grund lange von den Menschen gemieden wurden.

Der Südtiroler Schriftsteller und Ethnologe kroatischer Herkunft Karl Felix Wolff beschreibt diese Welt der Sagen und Mythen. Er hat diese Geschichten gesammelt und in einem umfangreichen Zyklus von Dolomitensagen veröffentlicht; Geschichten vom Königreich Fanes und der Königin Dolasilla, die die Tochter eines kriegerischen Königs war. Oder von Laurin, dem König der Zwerge, und seinem fantastischen Rosengarten, der im Herzen jener Berge lag, die auch heute noch Rosengarten genannt werden.

Die Zeit der ersten Besteigungen konnte den Zauber nicht brechen, den der Mensch um diese Berge gelegt hat, sondern brachte vielmehr neue Geschichten hervor, die, getragen vom alten Aberglauben, von den waghalsigen Abenteuern der ersten Bergpioniere erzählten. Die Dolomiten, die wegen ihrer außergewöhnlichen Entstehungsgeschichte ins Licht der Öffentlichkeit getreten sind, galten mit ihren noch unbezwungenen Gipfeln bald als Herausforderung, als Metapher für eine unbekannte Welt, als Prüfstein für Kraft und Willensstärke.

Die ersten Touristen in den Dolomiten waren vor allem englische und deutsche Bergsteiger. Sie knüpften mannigfach Kontakte zur einheimischen Bevölkerung — der Anfang einer traditionellen Gastfreundschaft. Erst in den darauffolgenden Jahrzehnten wandelte sie sich zur Dienstleistung und bildete so die Wurzeln für das Phänomen »Tourismus«. Die Namen dieser ersten Bergpioniere sind ein für allemal mit der Erschließungsgeschichte der Dolomiten verbunden. Dem Engländer John Ball, ein Wissenschaftler und Bergexperte, der 20 Jahre lang die Alpenkette erforscht hat, ist die Erstbesteigung des Monte Pelmo (1857) zuzuschreiben; begleitet wurde er von einem Gemsenjäger. Ein weiterer Angelsachse, Francis Fox Tuckett, erreichte 1867 den Gipfel der Civetta und bezwang 1872 als erster die Cima Brenta; 1863 bestieg der legendäre Wiener Dolomitenpionier Paul Grohmann die Tofana di Rozes, die Marmolada und den Piz Boè. Er war der Held des Jahres 1869, als er als Erster die Dreischusterspitze, die Große Zinne und den Langkofel bestieg. Weitere wichtige Gipfel wurden kurz hintereinander erobert: der Antelao, der Monte Cristallo, der Sorapis in den Ampezzaner Dolomiten, die Spitzen der Südtiroler Rosengartengruppe, die Pala di San Martino, die Gipfel der Brentagruppe im Trentino und schließlich die Civettagipfel in den Belluneser Dolomiten. Die meisten dieser denkwürdigen Unternehmungen waren bereits vor der Jahrhundertwende erfolgt. Sie wurden in fester Zusammenarbeit der angereisten Bergsteiger mit einheimischen Führern durchgeführt.

Die einzigartige Schönheit dieser Gebirgsregion, die so ganz anders ist als die der Gletscherberge in den Westalpen, wo die Pioniere des Alpinismus ihre ersten Siege errungen hatten, zog die Besucher wie ein Magnet an. Ihre Berühmtheit nahm ab der Mitte des 19. Jahrhunderts im Verlauf von nur wenigen Jahren enorm zu. Der Engländer John Ball bemerkte als einer der ersten Reisenden, die dieses Gebirge besucht haben: »... in keinem anderen Teil der Alpen erheben sich riesengroße Gipfel so abrupt und ohne jede Spur von Verbindung untereinander. Nirgendwo sonst gibt es so markante Kontraste, wie sie hier die geologische Struktur dem Reisenden bietet...«.

Solche ungewöhnlichen Charakterisierungen, ideal um Phantasie und Neugierde der ersten Reisenden anzuregen, die von Deutschland aus in das Tiroler Gebirge vordrangen, werden auch in dem 1837 vom Engländer Murray herausgegebenen Führer deutlich: »... es ist ganz anders als jedes andere Gebirge, in keinem anderen Teil der Alpen kann man dergleichen Berge beobachten. Sie ziehen wegen ihrer Einzigartigkeit, wegen des pittoresken Charakters ihrer Formen und wegen der Steilheit ihrer Bergspitzen, ja Nadeln, die Aufmerksamkeit auf sich ..., sie sind völlig ohne Vegetation und gewöhnlich von einer sanft gelben oder weißlichen Farbe. ... Nur diejenigen, die sie gesehen haben, sind in der Lage, sie gebührend zu schätzen.«

Im gleichen Maß wie die naturwissenschaftlichen Erkenntnisse und die Zahl der gewagten Erstbesteigungen zunahmen, wuchs auch der Mythos um diese Berge. Zeichnungen und Reiseskizzen, aber mehr noch die Tagebücher, Führer und ersten wissenschaftlichen Veröffentlichungen nährten das Interesse an den Dolomiten. Diese Fülle an Literatur fand in der schwärmerischen Beschreibung der eigenwilligen Schönheit der Landschaft und ihrer magischen Verbindung zu den Naturelementen ihr ständig wiederkehrendes Thema. Wir wollen uns an dieser Stelle mit einer poetischen Schilderung von Guido Rey begnügen:

»Das Tal ist völlig im Schatten versunken, aber ein undeutliches Leuchten taucht ganz oben im Dämmerlicht des Himmels auf und zieht den Blick auf sich: Alle Gipfel der Bergkette glühen noch, glühen sanft, von einer verborgenen Flamme genährt, wie wenn sie von einem inwendigen Feuer erleuchtet würden, das durch den Felsen hindurchscheint. Es ist ein ruhiges und starkes Licht, das keine Schatten wirft, keinen anderen Teil der Erde oder des Himmels erleuchtet, sondern nur die Gipfel in einen goldroten Bernsteinglanz einhüllt, ein Rot wie in schwankenden Baumkronen oder auf durchscheinenden Blättern in der Oktobersonne.«

Die Epoche der großen alpinistischen Erschließung erstreckt sich bis in das letzte Viertel des 19. Jahrhunderts. Der Eisenbahnbau über den Brennerpaß, der die natürliche Verbindung zum Mittelpunkt Europas herstellt, erleichtert den Zugang. Allmählich verlieren die Dolomiten ihre Aura von Mysterium und Legende. Der enorme internationale Bekanntheitsgrad erleichtert nun, das Gebiet direkt kennenzulernen; bald tauchen — noch vereinzelt — die ersten Zeichen des Tourismus auf, der durch die extra für den Gast geschaffenen Dienstleistungen gefördert wird: neue Paßstraßen, ein dichteres Netz von anspruchsvolleren Herbergen und, nicht zu vergessen, ortsansässige Führer, die den Bergsteigern zur Verfügung stehen! Nicht einmal der Erste Weltkrieg — der hier, im Grenzgebiet, die Dolomitengipfel in dramatischen Schlachten mit Furcht und Schrecken überzog — bremste den bemerkenswerten Touristenandrang nachhaltig. In kurzer Zeit erlangten die Hauptorte als Reiseziele internationales Niveau.

Dies war die Blütezeit für Cortina d'Ampezzo, das vom europäischen Großbürgertum zu einem seiner Hauptwohnsitze auserkoren wurde und ihm als exklusiver Ort mondäner Vergnügung diente. So also wurde dem Reigen der Attraktionen der Dolomiten eine weitere hinzugefügt — leider eine, die sich in Zukunft oft als zweischneidig erweisen sollte.

Mit dem Anwachsen des Tourismus intensivierten sich auch die Beziehungen zur Bevölkerung, den Ladinern aus Fassa, Gröden, Abtei, Fodom oder Ampezzo, deren jahrhundertealte Traditionen in einer stolzen Unabhängigkeit und tiefer Heimatverbundenheit wurzelten. Die Täler, die vom großen Sellastock abzweigen, wurden schon immer von diesem Bauernvolk bewohnt. Die alte Sprechweise dort unterscheidet sich von allen anderen Sprachen dieser Alpenregion. Die Ladiner siedelten dort in einem Gebiet, wo das Leben nichts mit »Normalität« oder »Sicherheit« zu tun hat. Gerade die beunruhigende Allgegenwart des Gebirges — feindselig und unberechenbar, oft der Ursprung von Gefahr und Tod — prägte die Menschen dort und formte jene »... einzigartige und faszinierende Kultur, die den gleichen Ursprung zu haben scheint wie der geologische Fortbestand der Korallen ... in der Kulturgeschichte ist sie eine ebenso große Ausnahmeerscheinung wie der Dolomit in der Naturgeschichte« (De Battaglia).

Das ladinische Volk ist sich seiner tiefen Wurzeln wohl bewußt; sie gehen auf rhätische Völkerschaften zurück, die sich einst hier niederließen. Ihre ethnischen Eigenarten haben sich dann mit denen der nordischen Völker vermischt, die zwischen dem fünften und achten Jahrhundert die Alpen überquerten, um die Poebene zu erobern. In dieser historischen Phase verfestigt sich die Entstehungsgeschichte dieses Volkes, das wegen seiner wirtschaftlichen und geographischen Isolation wohlbehütet durch die darauffolgenden Jahrhunderte kommt. Die Abgeschiedenheit ist der Hauptgrund für seine ungebrochene kulturelle Identität, die auch heute noch besteht; eine Kontinuität, die die Natur- und Kulturlandschaft ihres Lebensraums gleichermaßen erhalten hat. Aus diesem Grund »... fordern diese Menschen, genauso wie die Felsen ringsum, Respekt; nicht um 'beschützt' zu werden, sondern um auch weiterhin auf ihren alten, gewachsenen Wegen in die Zukunft gehen zu können. Die Ladiner sind keine Minderheit, die nur von folkloristischem Interesse ist; sie sind eine große und einzigartige Kultur ...« (De Battaglia).

Von Dolomieu bis heute sind 200 geschichtsträchtige Jahre vergangen, und wir stehen nunmehr an der Schwelle zum nächsten Jahrtausend. In heutiger Zeit eröffnen sich neue Perspektiven über den Felskämmen der Dolomiten: Die wissenschaftliche Erforschung ihrer geologischen Zusammensetzung zielt nun darauf ab, über das Verständnis der Herkunft und Entstehung jener so markanten Felsformationen hinaus einen neuen technologischen Ansatz zur Erdölsuche zu finden. Neue Ziele erfordern neue Methoden ...

Wenn man anläßlich dieses zweihundertsten Jahrestages Teile der Geschichte neu bewertet, so muß dies für die Zukunft Auswirkungen auf unsere Beziehung zu den Dolomiten und unserem Verhalten dort haben. Die Auseinandersetzung mit der Vergangenheit sollte nicht nur die rein geographische Kenntnis der Dolomiten fördern, sondern uns bewußt machen, was sie in unserem täglichen Leben bedeuten können. Hier, zwischen den roten Zinnen, auf den Gipfeln oder an den Hängen der Massive, kann man seiner Phantasie noch freien Lauf lassen, kann man auf Dolasilla, die Königin von Fanes treffen oder den Rosengarten von König Laurin erblicken. Vielleicht belohnt die reine Natur nur den damit, zu sich selbst zu finden, der sich ihr mit seiner ganzen Aufmerksamkeit nähert. Hierzu abschließend ein Wort von Severino Casara: »Ich kann mich nicht an die Einsamkeit der Geburt erinnern und kenne auch nicht die des Todes, aber ich meine, die Einsamkeit des Lebens verstanden zu haben in dieser erhabenen Berührung mit der Natur, eben dort oben. . . . Du begreifst, daß das Leben nur eine kurze körperliche Durchreise auf der Erde ist, der Geist hingegen stirbt nicht.«

Not so long ago, I embarked on an unusual experiment. I asked a fair number of persons whether they knew the Dolomites. Everyone — whether Italians or foreigners — came out with an unqualified, unhesitating »yes«. When I put a second question, however, namely »Where are these renowned mountains situated«, the mists of doubt began to form. Hardly anyone was able to pinpoint the correct localities and provinces, and several people tried desperately to make the best of a bad job with such tentative liaisons as: »next to Venice . . . in der Nähe von Gardasee . . . in Sudtirolo . . . nel Trentino . . ., no, tra Bolzano e l'Austria«, and other limping approximations.

My experiment was thus a success and its message crystal-clear. The international fame of these peaks goes hand in hand with but vague notions as to their proper place on the map. Not that I blame my interviewees. Even so, the significance of their varied answers lies in the confirmation of an often absent match between renown und accuracy. And, of course, the position has been worse confounded in recent years by a body of literature prepared for hikers and those with an interest in nature and geology, which, while vast and constantly updated, has resulted in false attributions to one province rather than another, overlooking the fact that mountains, like other natural environments, form a common heritage unbridled by man-made boundaries.

In the spirit of this common patrimony, two hundred years since the entry of their mountains into the realm of science as the Dolomites, the people of these valleys have sought to place, in various ways, the correct emphasis on a bicentenary that also recalls the birth of a spirit of exploration of its own domains by an enlightened Europe.

Fame, therefore, still clings to this »recent« discovery, for it was in 1788 that the French geologist Déodat Tancred de Dolomieu first defined the peculiar features of the rock that bears his name. Indeed, it was this initial journey of his among the mountains with their »unique, unreal appearance«, that marked the start of a fortune based on a growing interest in their natural beauty, and as an ideal place for mountaineers and hikers alike.

Moreover, it is indeed their geological confirmation that sets the limits of the Dolomites — an Alpine chain, broadly divided into an Eastern and a Western part, that lies in the Provinces of Belluno, Bolzano and Trento, and is bounded by the rivers Adige, Isarco, Piave, Rienza, Cismon and Brenta. The term also embraces the extensive massif of the Brenta Group in the Trentino between the Adige, the Sarca and the Noce, as well as the Little Dolomites, a ridge linking the Lessini und Pasubio Groups in the pre-Alpine region of the Veneto.

Dolomieu's »discovery« served to confer a different lease of life on these marvellous stone colossi, one to add to that inner live whereby they are rendered a glowing red when the sun's last rays play over their rough surfaces, or a lunar white in the night hours, hence their original name: the »Pale Mountains«. For their true birth, on the other hand, we must look 250 million years ago, when an eruptive episode created a sea peopled by organisms whose layered growth resulted in the formation of huge coral reefs, rendered more evident by glacial degradation after the waters receded. The complex geological phenomena are still in progress and do not need to be explained here. Suffice it to say that since the judgement initially expressed by Dolomieu: »... this is a very poorly effervescent limestone rock that surrounds and in many cases covers the granite mountains between Trento and Bolzano«, they have been the subject of continuous study.

The secrets of Mont Blanc and the Western Alps were quickly unravelled in the early 1800's. As the century proceeded, therefore, there was a growing interest in the Dolomites and a desire to known more about them. The direct knowledge increasingly provided by these early explorers and researchers naturally encouraged a flow of other visitors and slowly helped to confer on this fascinating highland landscape the special »je ne sais quoi« that even now clings to its name.

True stories and legends are intricately interwoven in this corner of the Alps, a world anchored to its superstitions, peopled by presences both fantastic and divine, the source of a form of reverential fear of these so long untrodden peaks. A universe described by the ethnologist and writer Karl Felix Wolff, a Sud-Tyrolean of Croat descent, who collected and published an extensive cycle of legends with a Dolomite setting. Tales of the realm of the Fanes and Queen Dolasilla, daughter of its warlike monarch; of Laurino, king of the dwarves, and his fantastic rose garden in the heart of the Catinaccio (still called the Rosengarten in German).

A flurry of first ascents, what is more, did not break the spell men had woven around these mountains, but provided the raw material for other legends resting on a far more solid substratum of truth associated with the daring deeds of the pioneers of mountaineering. Brought into the limelight on account of their extraordinary natural history, the Dolomites were soon to be viewed as a challenge with their inviolate peaks, the metaphor for an unknown world, a proving ground for strenght and determination.

British and German climbers were the main forerunners in this opening up of the Dolomite valleys. They readily established good relations with the local people and thus set in motion a process whereby a tradition for hospitality was created, services were changed and expanded, and the seeds of modern tourism were sown.

A handful of names will suffice to tell the tale. John Ball, an English scientist and expert mountaineer, who explored and studied the Alpine chains for twenty years and was the first to reach the top of Monte Pelmo in 1857 in the company of a chamois hunter. Francis Fox Tuckett, another British climber, who scaled the Civetta in 1867, the Brenta in 1872, and the Rosengarten in 1874. The ever-busy Viennese devourer of peaks, Paul Grohmann, a legend unto himself. The Tofana di Rozes, the Marmolada and the Piz Boè succumbed to his talents in 1863, and six years later he performed another hat-trick by dismissing the Dreischuster Spitz, the Cima Grande di Lavaredo, and the Langkofel.

One by one, all the other main summits felt the tread of human footsteps: Antelao, Cristallo and Sorapiss in the Ampezzo Dolomites, the Rosengarten cluster in the Alto Adige Dolomites, the Brenta Group in the Trentino and the civetta Group in the Belluno Dolomites.

These were memorable exploits, the most outstanding being completed during the closing years of the century in a camaraderie between climbers and local guides that marked one of the most exalted features of man's relationship with the mountains. The singular beauty of these peaks, so different from the Swiss glaciers and the Western Alps where the pioneers of mountaineering achieved their first victories, provided a further magnet to draw visitors to the Dolomites. Their fame thus grew enormously and apace after the middle of the 19th century. In the words of John Ball, one of their earliest admirers: »... in no other part of the Alps do such tall peaks rear up so brusquely and with no apparent links between them. Nowhere else are there such marked contrasts stemming from differences in geological structure as those that here strike the visitor ...«.

These unusual features, an ideal spur to the phantasy and desire for knowledge of the first visitors to thrust down frim Germany to the Tyrol, are equally evident in the chapter on the Dolomites in the guide to the Alps prepared by the English publisher Murray in 1837: »... different from every other mountain, it is not given to view their likes in any other part of the Alps. They attract attention on account of the singularity and picturesque character of their shapes, their sharp peaks and needles ... bare, devoid of vegetation of any kind, and usually of a slight yellow or off white hue.... Only those who have seen them are capable of appreciating them as they deserve«.

The myth has thus lived on through new geological and naturalistic discoveries, and the bold enterprises of these pioneers. Yet even more through drawings and sketches made by travellers, and above all their diaries, along with the first guides and scientific publications that nurtured a mounting interest in the Dolomites, and sparked off a wealth of writings whose »leitmotivs« were the beauties of the landscape and its magical combinations of natural features.

Let us content ourselves with this poetic description by Guido Rey: »The valley is all bathed in shadows, but an indefinite glow still haunts the twilight sky and will not be denied. All the peaks are still aglow with the gentle fires of a hidden flame, as though illuminated by an inner incandescence transpiring through the stone. A calm, potent light that neither generates shadows nor lends its rays to any other part of the earth or the sky, but solely swathes the peaks in red gilded with ancient amber, the red of dancing tree-tops or diaphanous leaves under an October sky«.

Epic ascents continued to fill the headlines in the last quarter of the century. Easier access was provided by the construction of the Brenner railway link to Central Europe. Breezy familiarity thus slowly stripped the Dolomites of their aura of mystery and legend. Facts and figures were extensively published throughout the world and formed the basis for a direct contact. Fledging tourism appeared, encouraged by various services set up to attract visitors: new roads through the valleys, better and more appropriate hotels and accommodation in general, guides to show the way to climbers and simple walkers alike.

Not even the upheavals of the first world war, which engulfed the peaks of this frontier region in fierce and dramatic battles, placed a serious brake on a burgeoning tourism that quickly raised the main towns in the Dolomite valleys to the rank of synonyms for as many internationally renowned resorts. This was the time when Cortina came to the fore, chosen »nem. con.« by the wealthy bourgeoisie of Europe as a permanent port of call, an excusive rendezvous where worldly tourists could meet others of their kind. Thus was added another string to the Dolomites' bow of attractions, one that was unfortunately to prove more akin to a two-edged sword.

Increased tourism also intensified relations with the local Ladin folk of Fassa, Gardena, Badia, Fodom and Ampezzo, whose age-old traditions were based on proud independence and indissoluble links with their lands. The valleys branching off from the great massif of the Sella have always been inhabited by this peasant stock, whose ancient vernacular is in sharp contrast with the other languages spoken in this part of the Alps. They have settled an area where nothing is geared to »normalcy« or the »certainties« of life. Brooding mountains, hostile, unpredictable and of the source of peril and death, make every effort the outcome of a focussed, pondered decision, form the essential nature of a person's character, and define that »singular, fascinating culture that seems to be on the same footing as the geological continuity of the corals ... as exceptional on the pages of history as dolomite on the archives of Nature« (De Battaglia).

The Ladins are aware of their remote descent from Rhaetic folk who settled here and later blended with the Northmen whose invasions of the Po Valley led them through the Alps from the 5th to the 8th century. A genesis thereafter preserved by a geographical and economic isolation primarily responsible for an unbroken continuity of tradition from one generation to another that still persists in our time, a continuity whose meaning equally embraces both preservation of the natural and human landscape. It is for this very reason that »these people, like the rocks that surround them, demand respect, not to ensure their protection, but to enable them to continue to pass on their ancient ways to new, unpredictable centuries. The Ladins are not merely a minority of interest to folklorists, but a great, irrepeatable culture« (De Battaglia).

Two centuries of history bridge the gap between Dolomieu and our own times and form a prologue to the next millenium. New perspectives have been drawn on the rocky ridges of the Dolomites. Research on their geological composition is aimed at providing a contribution to the elaboration of oil prospecting technologies through an understanding of the origin of the ancient reefs and shelves that are such a feature of the landscape. New objectives lined to new requirements.

Fragments of history re-asserted on the occasion of this bicentenary have also determined the relationships and rules of behaviour for the future. Comparison with the past must in any event augment our knowledge of the Dolomites and this, as stated at the outset, goes beyond mere geography to the much more real consideration of what they represent in our daily lives. Here, among the red crags behind the peaks or on the slopes of the massifs, fancy is still free to roam. You can keep your tryst with Queen Dolasilla, or glimpse King Laurino's rose-bedecked bowers. With true Nature alone as their ambassador, those who succeed in approaching with due attention may perhaps be rewarded by the rediscovery of themselves. In the words of S. Casara: »I cannot recall the solitude of birth, nor ken I that of death. Yet I feel I have come to known the solitude of life in these sublime contacts with Nature. Up there ... you realise that life is a brief physical passage on earth, whereas the spirit dies not«.

Fotos von · photographs by
Attilio Boccazzi-Varotto

1.

1. Blick vom Karerpaß auf den Rosengarten.
   Passo di Costalunga. Gruppo del Catinaccio.
   Перевал Косталунга. Группа гор Катиначчио.
   コスタルンガ峠。　カティナッチョ山群

2. Fischleintal. Fischleinboden und Zwölferkofel.
   Val Fiscalina. Campo Fiscalino, Croda dei Toni.
   Долина Фискалина. Плац Фискалино и Крода дей Тони.
   フィスカリーナ谷。　カンポ・フィスカリーナとクローダ・ディ・トーニ

3. Innerfeldtal und Dreischusterspitze.
   Val Campo di Dentro. Cima Tre Scarperi.
   Валь Кампо ди Дентро. Вершина Тре Скарпери.
   カンポ・ディ・デーントロ谷。
   チーマ・トレ・スカルペリ

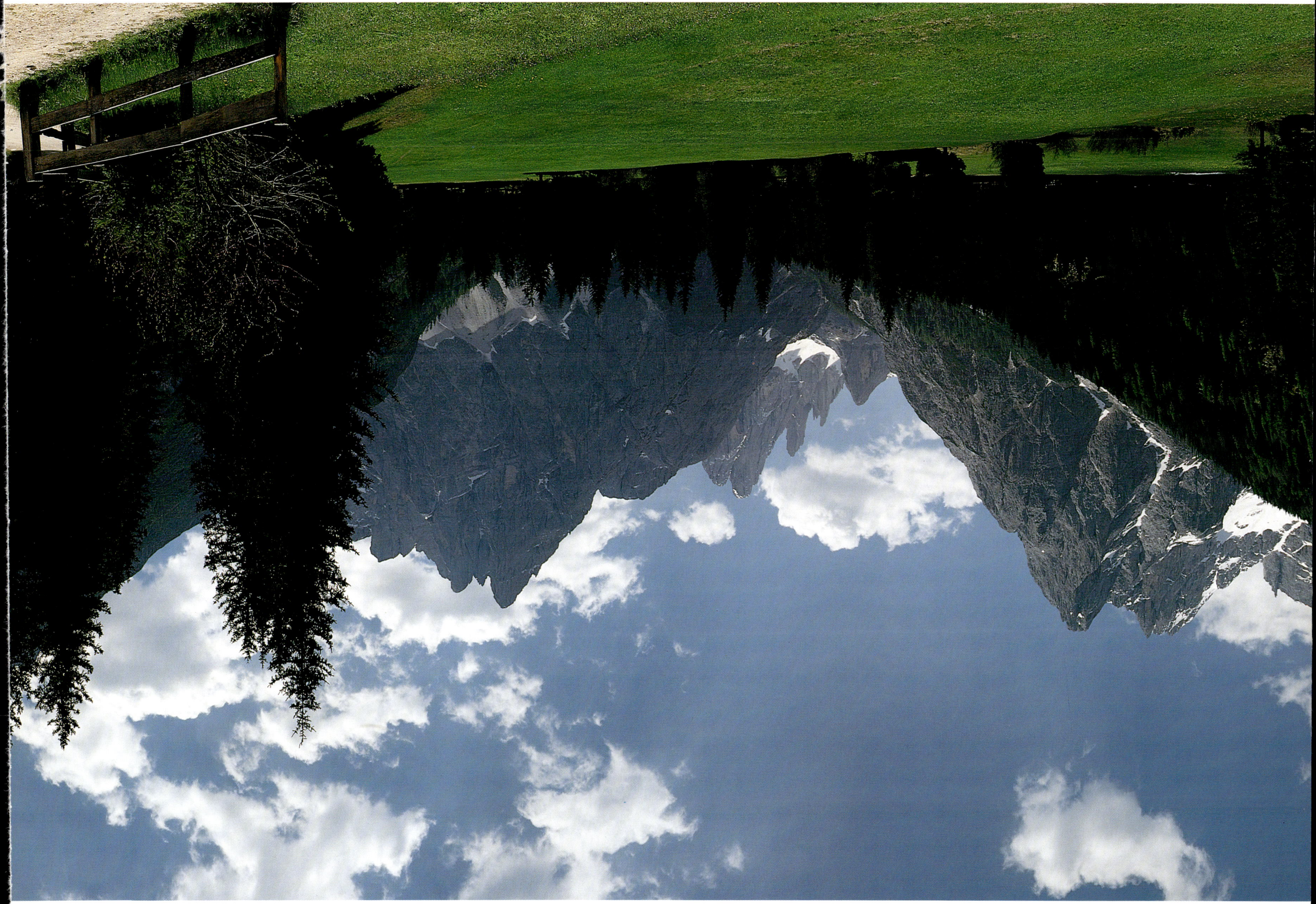

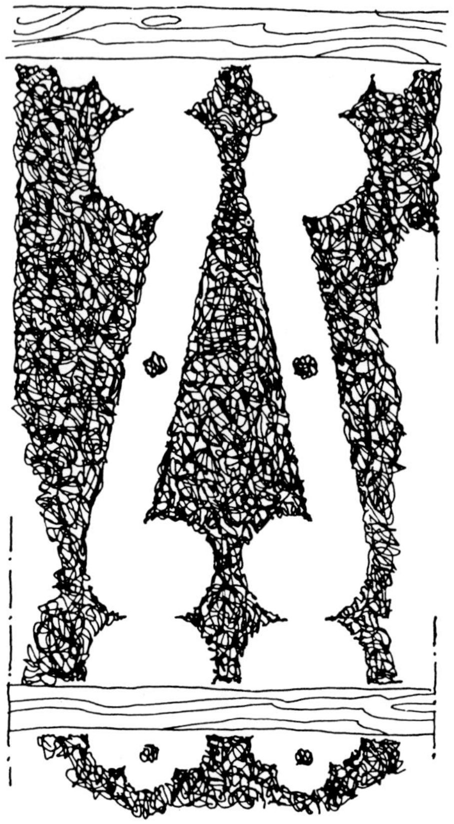

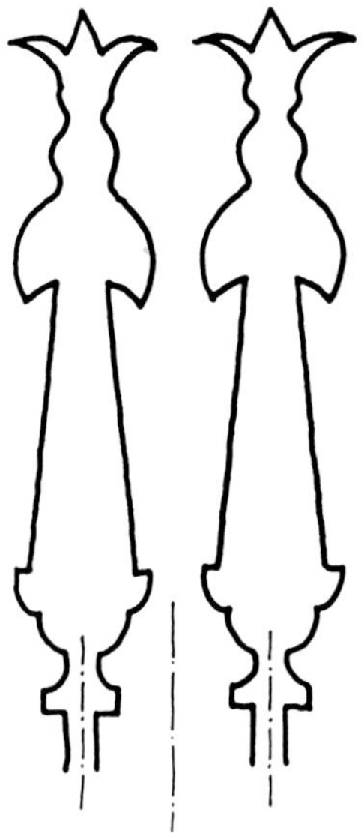

Ornamente und Ziermotive hölzerner Wandverkleidungen in der ländlichen Architektur des Abteitals

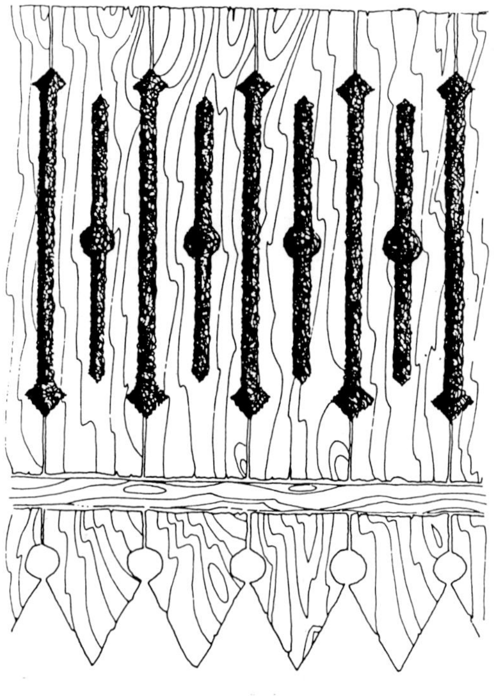

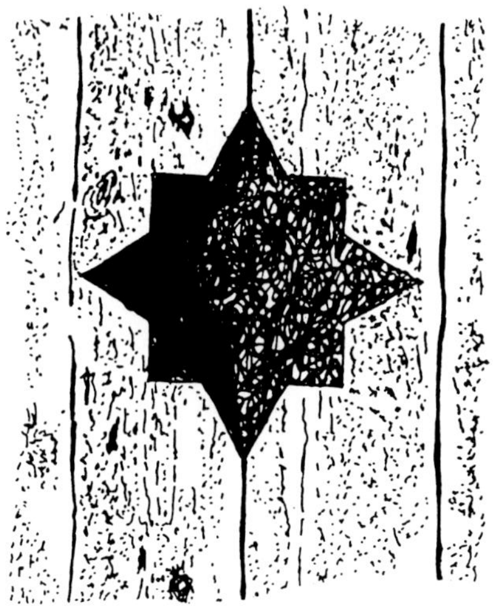

Holz in der Architektur
Balkone und Belüftungsluken an Heustadeln mit geometrischen Motiven

4.

4. Kapelle auf der Sennes-Alpe.
Cappella di Sènnes.
Sènnes Chapel.
Chapelle de Sènnes.
Capilla de Sènnes.
Капелла ди Сеѣннс.
センネスのチャペル

5. Pragser Wildsee und Seekofel.
   Lago di Bràies, Croda del Becco.
   Озеро Брайс и Крода дель Бекко.
   ブライエス湖とクローダ・デル・ベッコ

6. Blick von Misurina auf Marmarole und Sorapis.
   Misurina. Marmarole, Sorapiss.
   Мизурина. Мармароле и Сорапис.
   ミズリーナ。　マルマローレとソラピッス

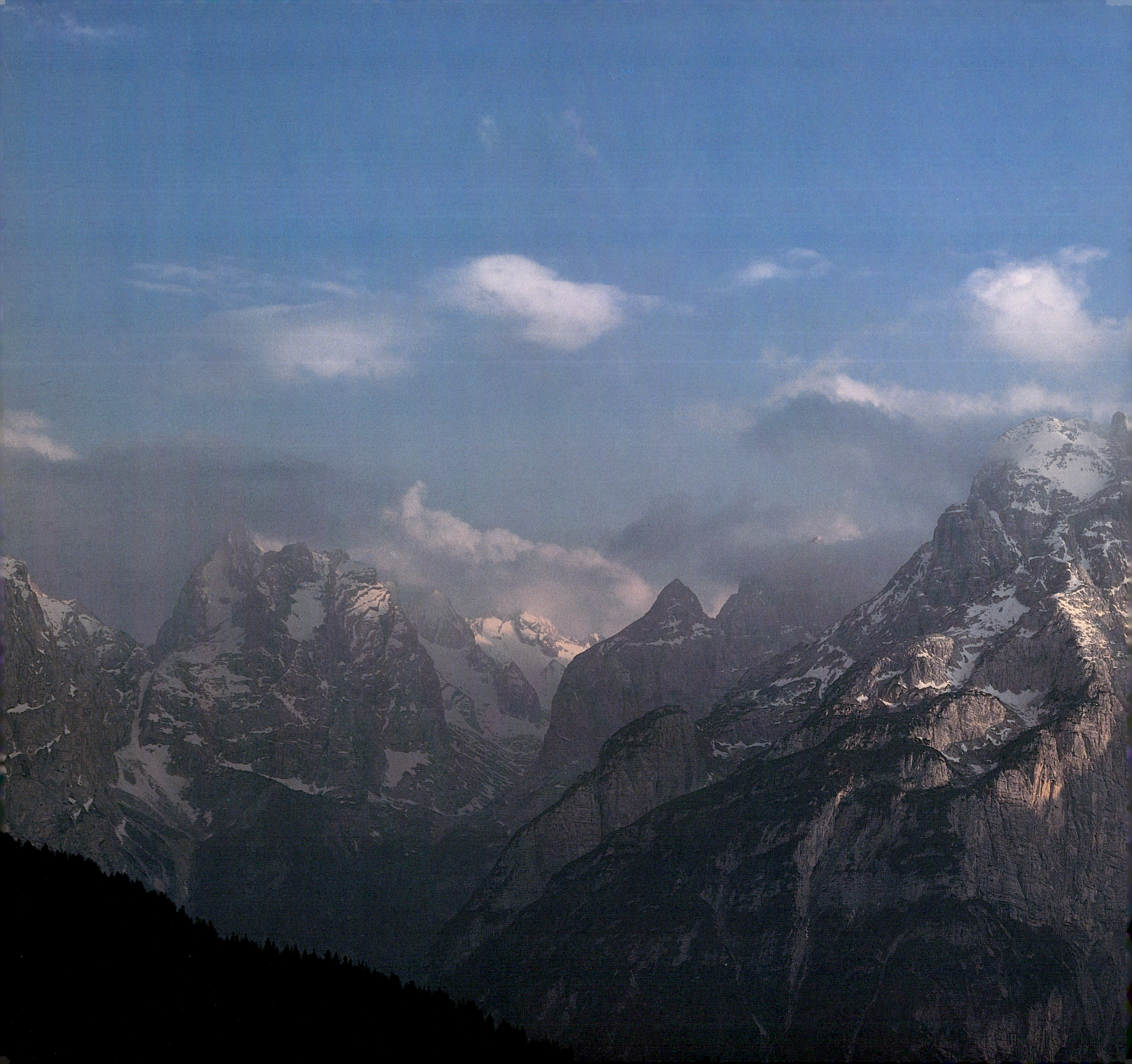

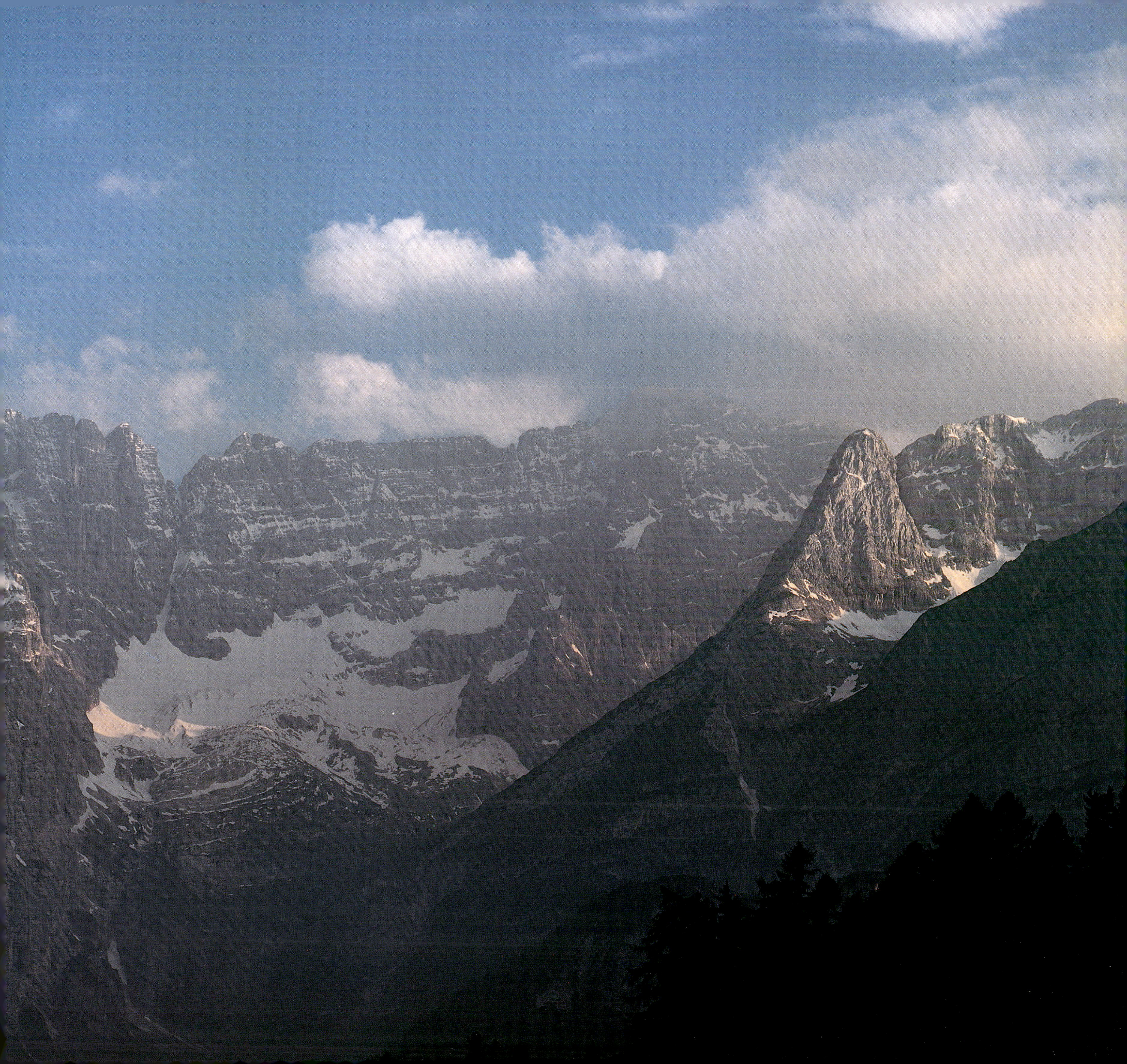

7. Dürrensee mit Cristallo-Gruppe.
   Lago di Landro. Gruppo del Cristallo.
   Озеро Ландро. Группа Хрустальных гор.
   ラーンドロ湖。　クリスタッロ山群

8. Cristallino und Piz Popena in der Cristallo-Gruppe.
   Gruppo del Cristallo. Cristallino, Piz Popena.
   Группа Хрустальных гор. Кристаллино и Пиц Попена.
   クリスタッロ山群。　クリスタッリーノとピッツ・ポペーナ

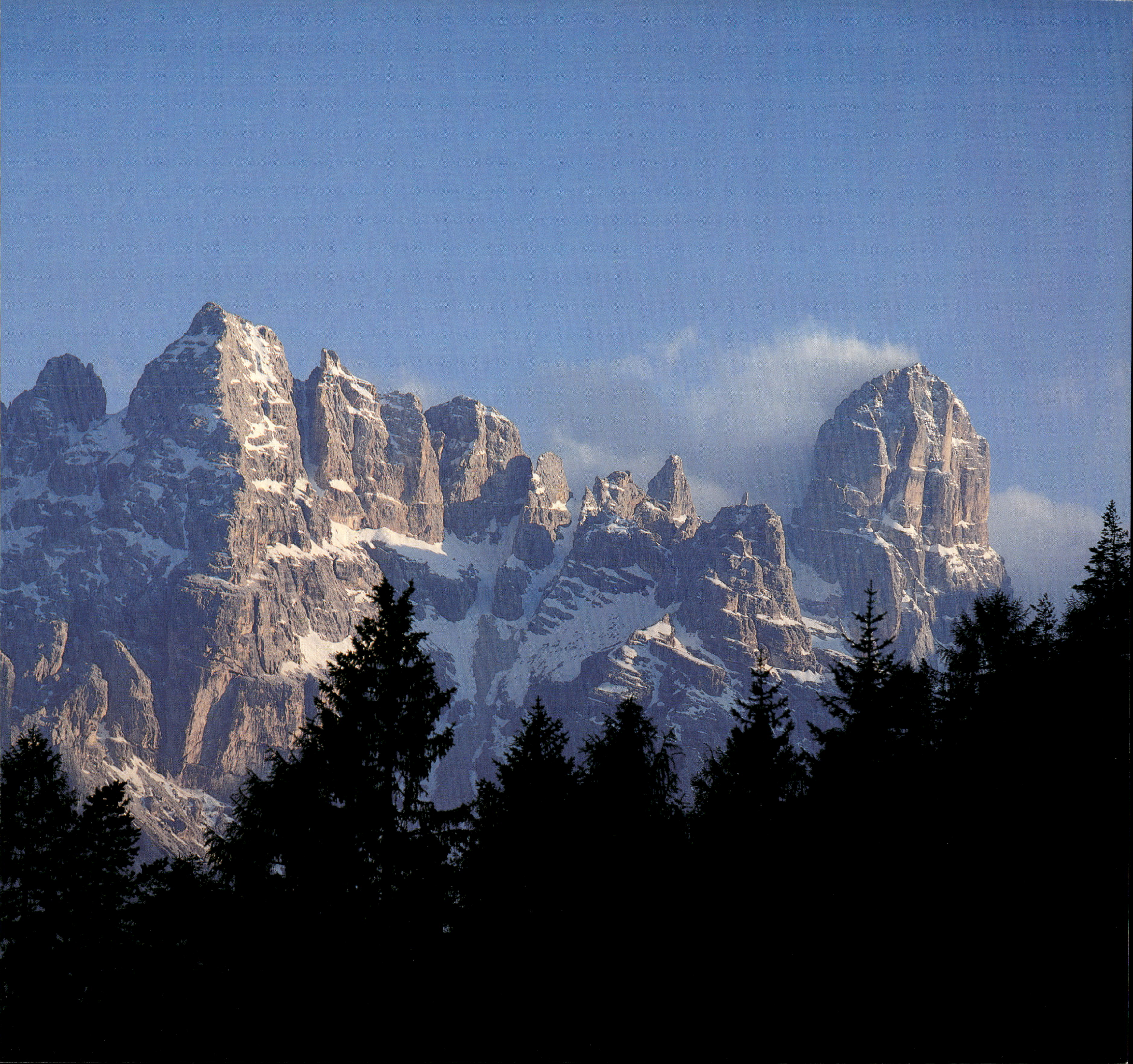

9.

9. In einer Almhütte.
   Interno di malga.
   Interior of a mountain hut.
   Intérieur d'alpage.
   Interior de choza de pastores.
   Интерьер пастушьей хижины в горах.
   マールガ（放牧小屋）の内部

10. Croda Marcora von San Vito di Cadore aus gesehen.
    San Vito di Cadore. Croda Marcòra.
    Сан Вито ди Кадорэ. Крода Маркора.
    サン・ヴィート・ディ・カドーレ。　クローダ・マールコラ

11. Monte Pelmo von Borca di Cadore aus gesehen.
    Borca di Cadore. Monte Pelmo.
    Борка ди Кадоре. Гора Пельмо.
    ボルカ・ディ・カドーレ。　モンテ・ペールモ

12. Santa Fosca im Fiorentinatal mit Marmolada.
    Val Fiorentina. Santa Fosca, Marmolada.
    Долина Фьорентина. Санта Фоска и Мармолада.
    フィオレンティーナ谷。
    サンタ・フォースカとマルモラーダ

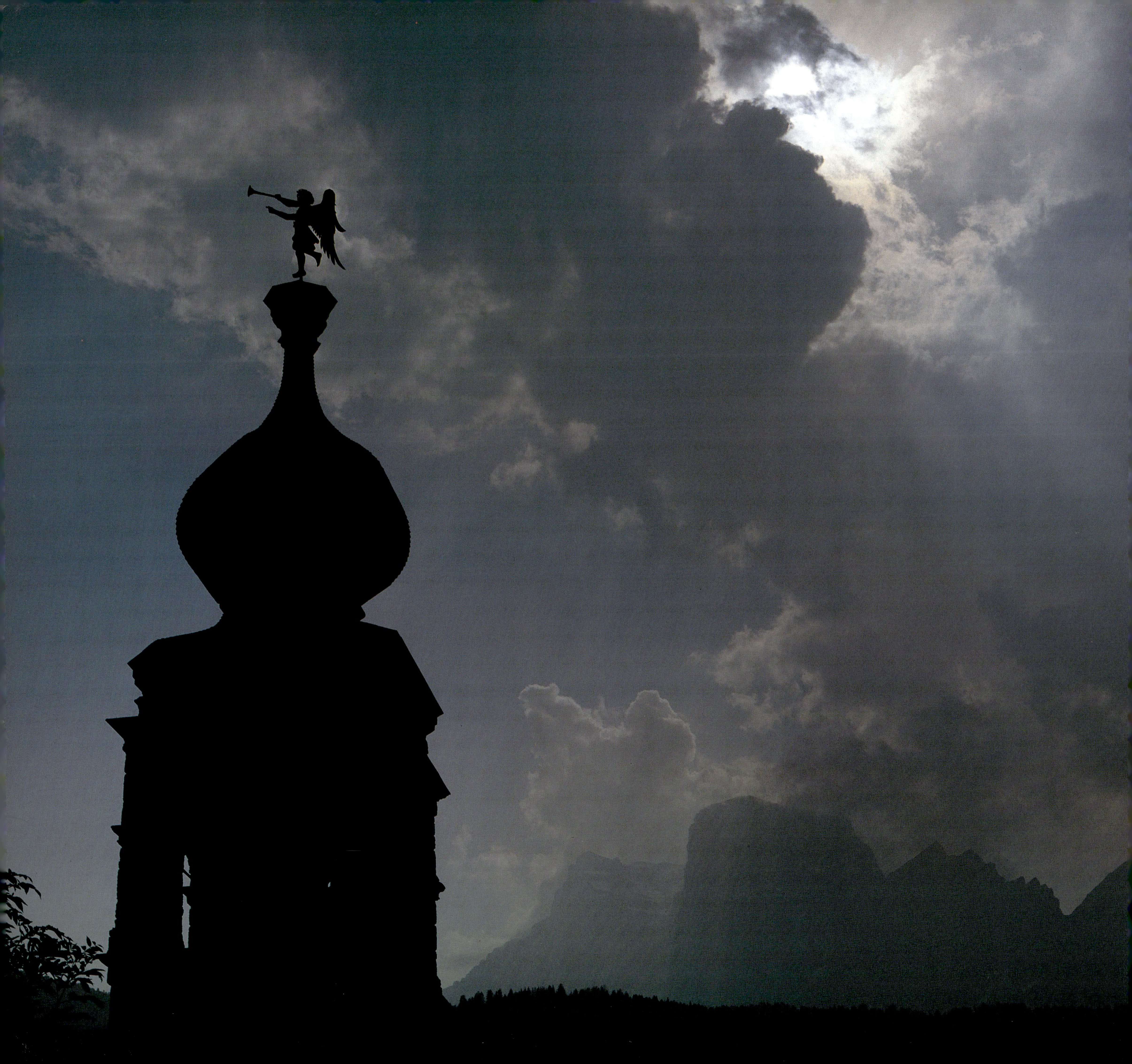

11.
12.

13. Fiorentinatal. Monte Pelmo.
Val Fiorentina. Monte Pelmo.
Долина Фиорентина. Гора Пельмо.
フィオレンティーナ谷。モンテ・ペールモ

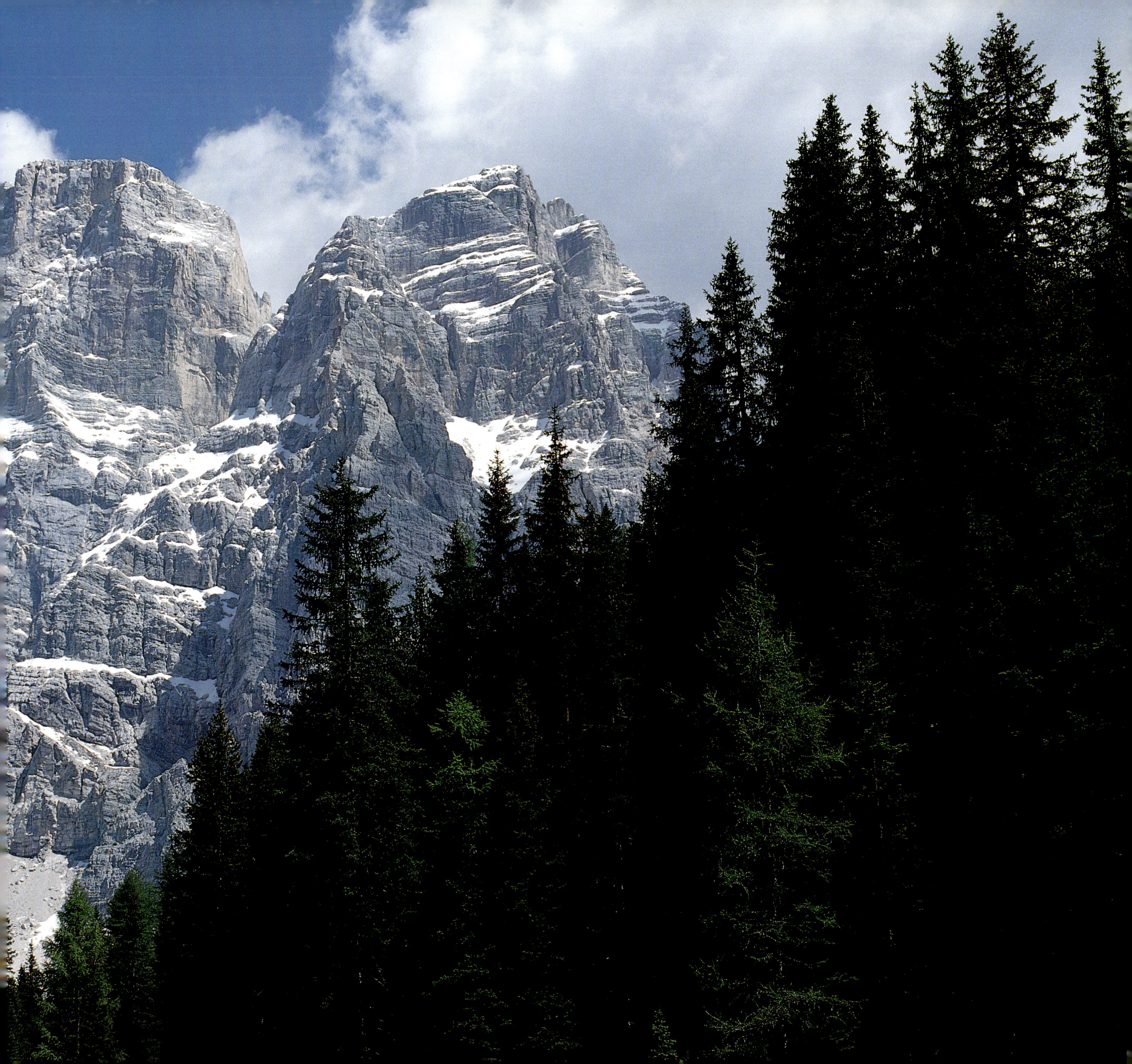

14. Auf der Alm in Fodara Vedla.
Alpeggio a Fodàra Vedla.
Alpine pastures at Fodàra Vedla.
Alpage à Fodàra Vedla.
Pastura en Fodàra Vedla.
Альпийские пастбища в Фодарэ Ведия.
フォダーレ・ヴェードゥラの放牧小屋

15. Ruine Andraz.
Castello di Andràz.
Andràz Castle.
Château d'Andràz.
Castillo de Andràz.
Костел Андрац.
アンドゥラッツの城

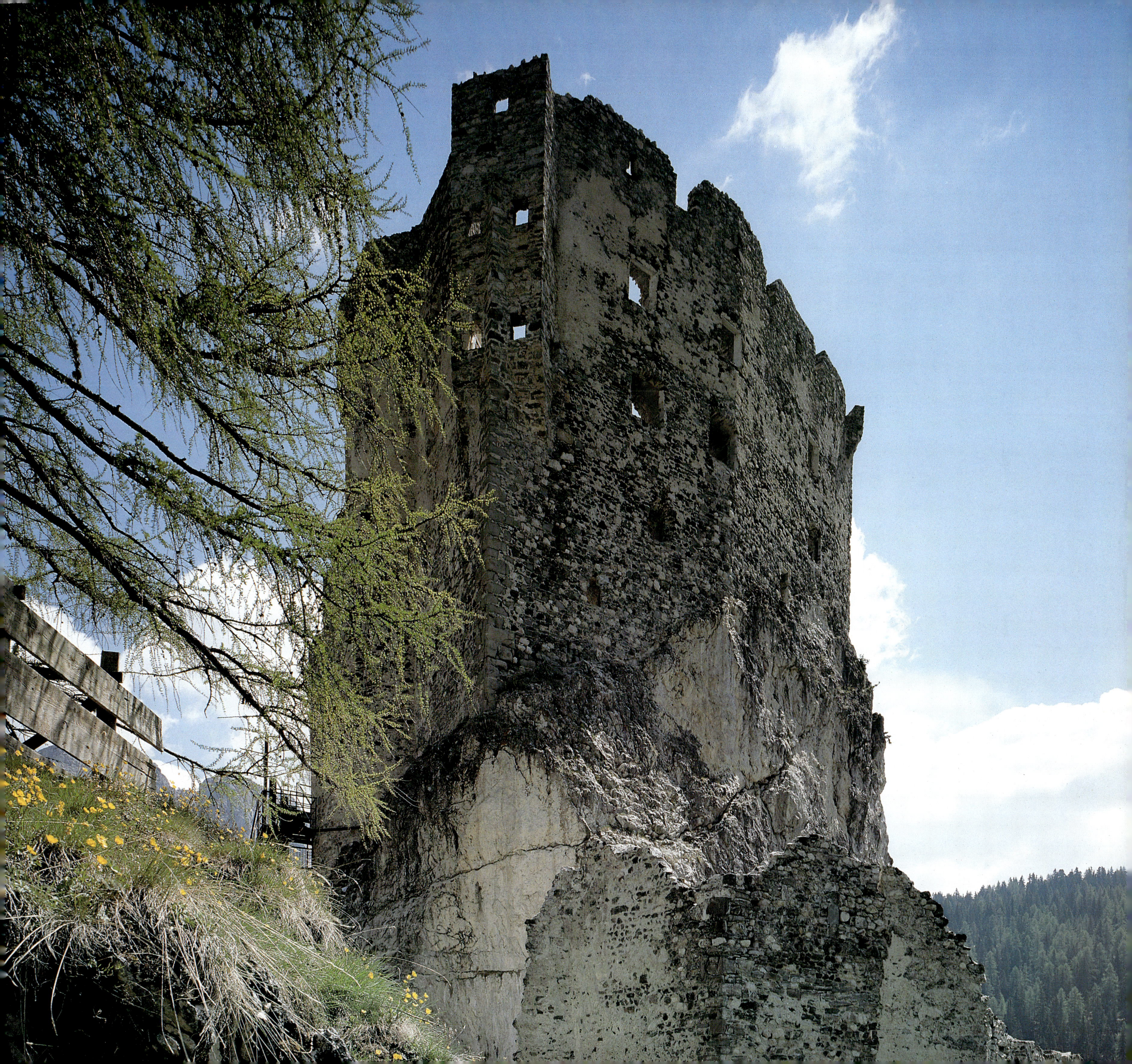

16.

16. Die Wände von Larséc bei Soraga im Fassatal.
Val di Fassa. Soràga, Dirupi di Larséch.
Долина Фасса. Сорага и Обрывы Ларсек.
ファッサ谷。　ソラーガとディルーピ・ディ・ラールセック

17. Blick auf Langkofel und Sella von der Pordoispitze aus.
Sass Pordoi. Veduta sui gruppi del Sassolungo e del Sella.
Sass Pordoi. The Sassolungo and Sella Groups.
Sass Pordoi. Vue sur les groupes du Sassolungo et du Sella.
Sass Pordoi. Vista de los grupos del Sassolungo y del Sella.
Сасс Пордой. Вид на группу Сассолунго и Сэлла.
サッス・ポルドーイ。　サッソ・ルンゴ山群

18. Karersee mit Latemar.
Lago di Carezza, Latemàr.
Озеро Карецца и Латемар.
カレッツア湖に映るラーテマル

19. Rosengarten und Latemar vom Nigersattel.
Passo Nigra. Catinaccio, Latemàr.
Перевал Нигра. Катиначчио и Латемар.
ニーグラ峠。　カティナッチョとラーテマル

17.

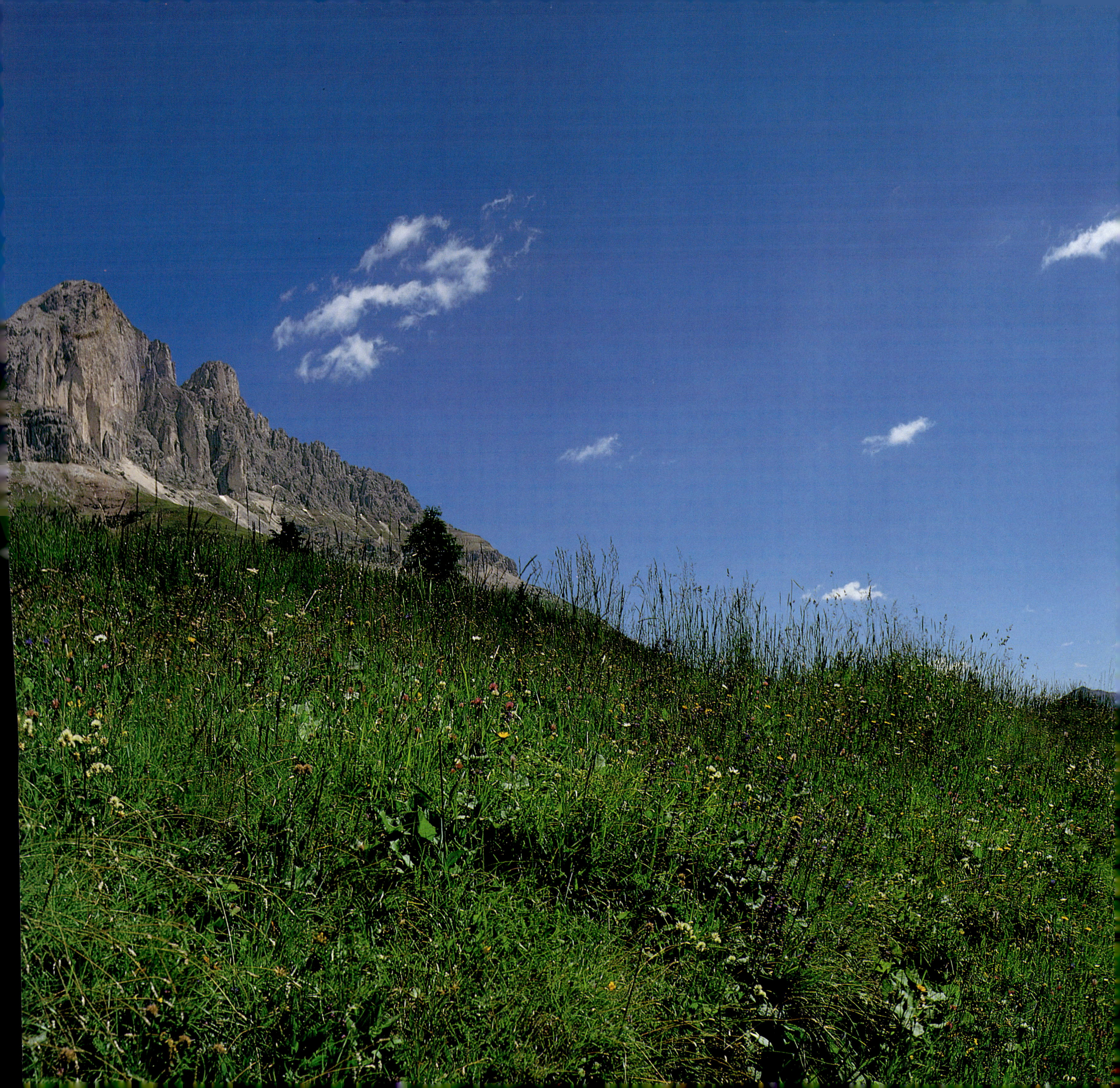

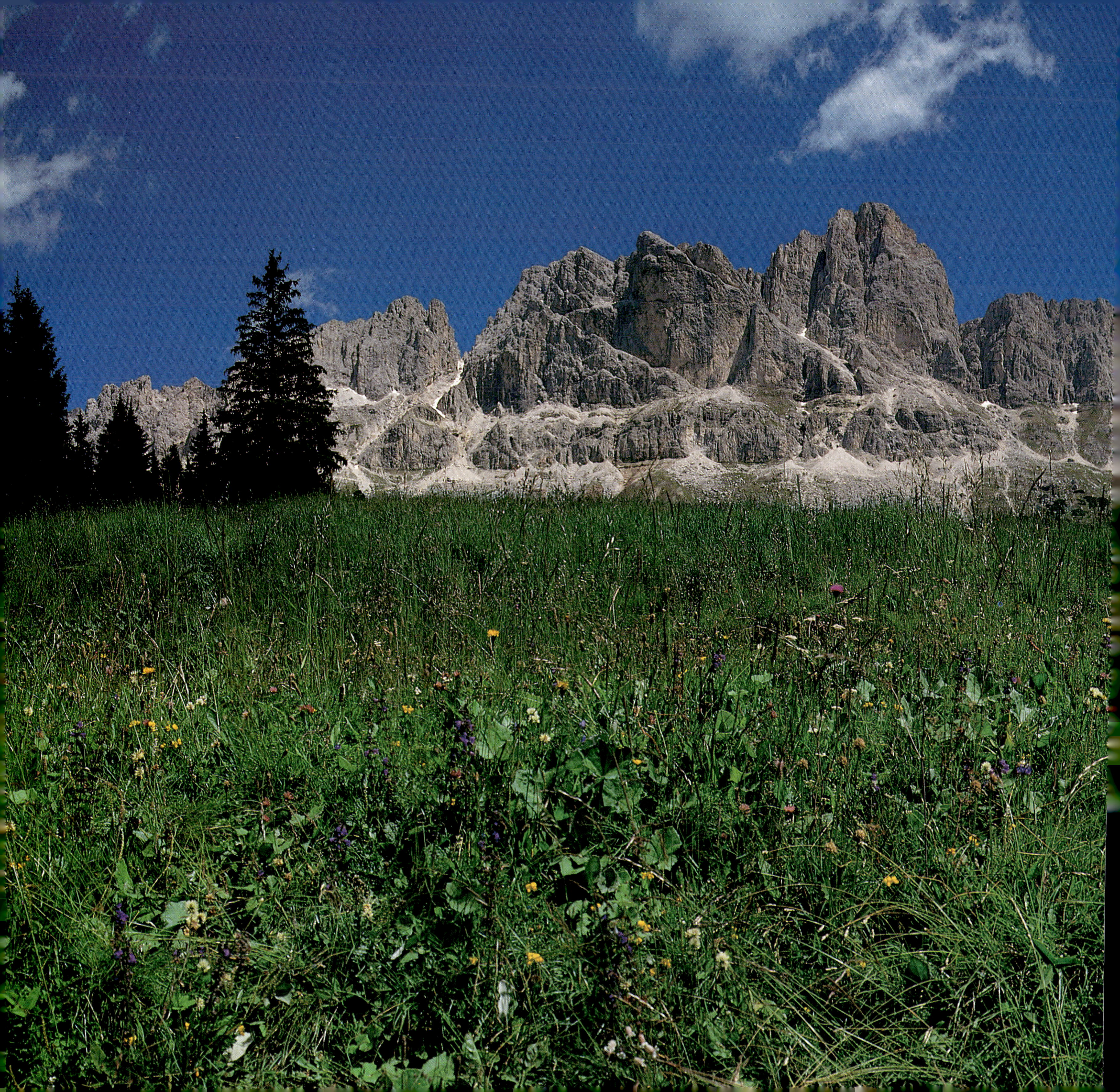

8.

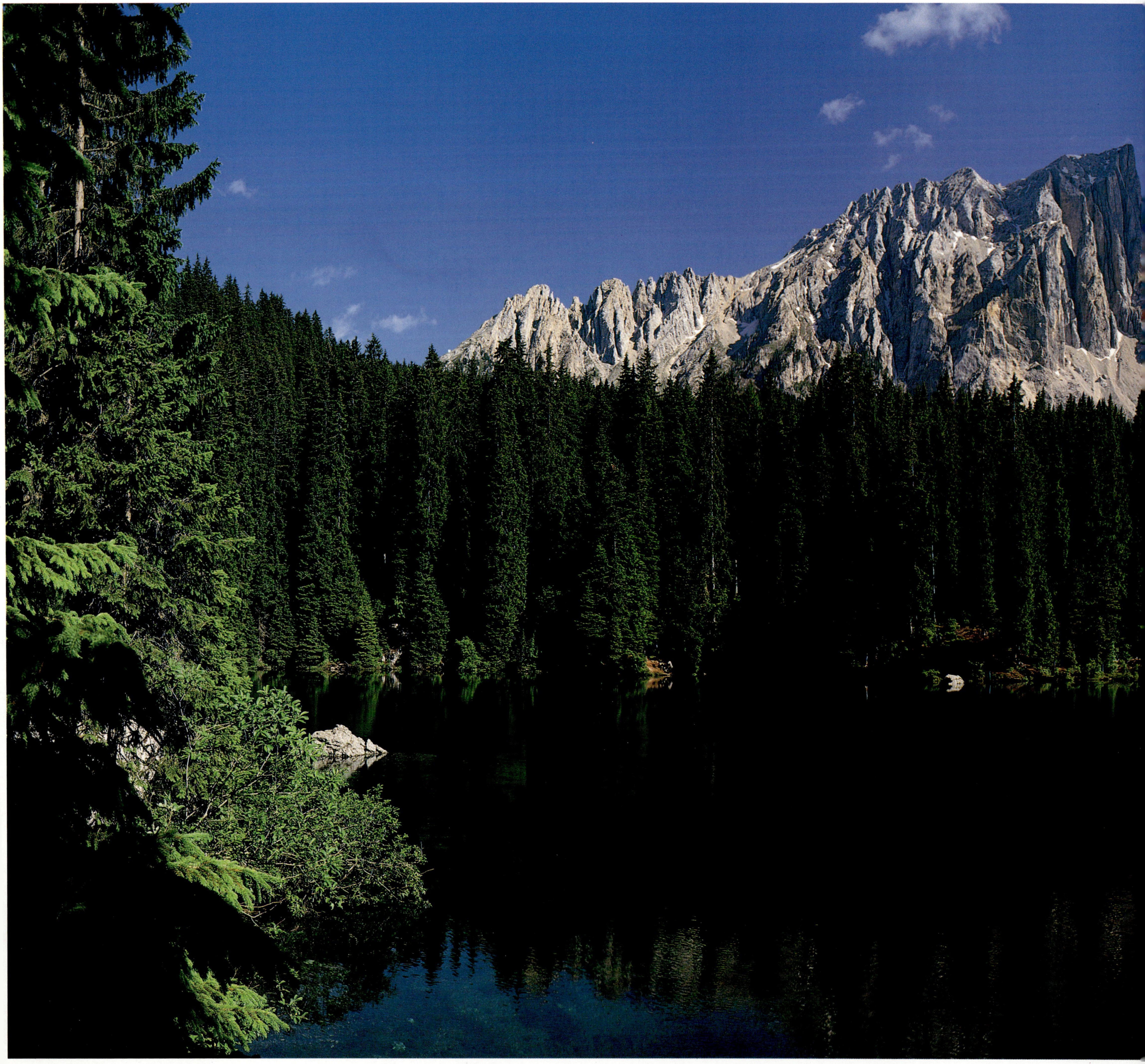

19.▸

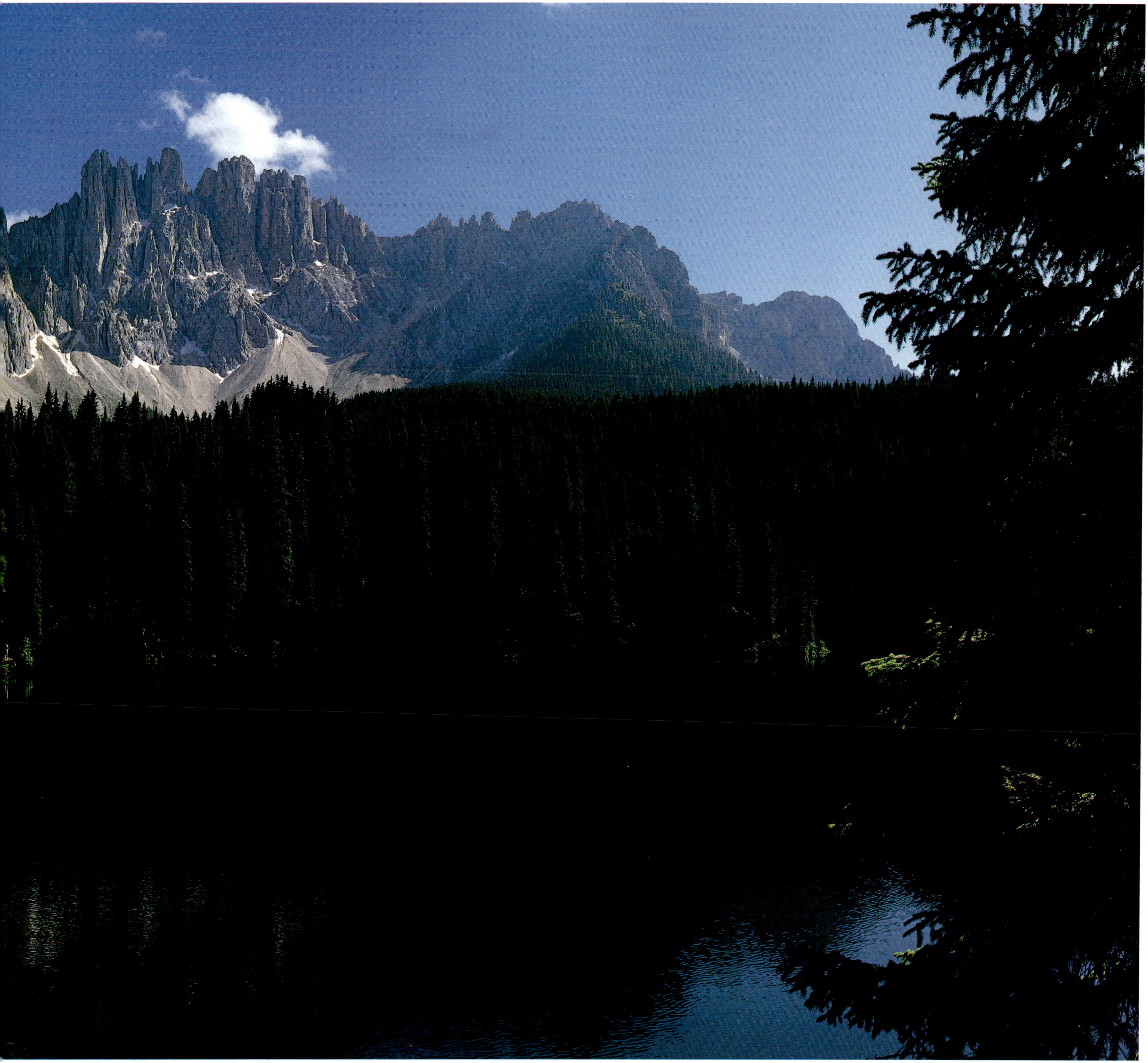

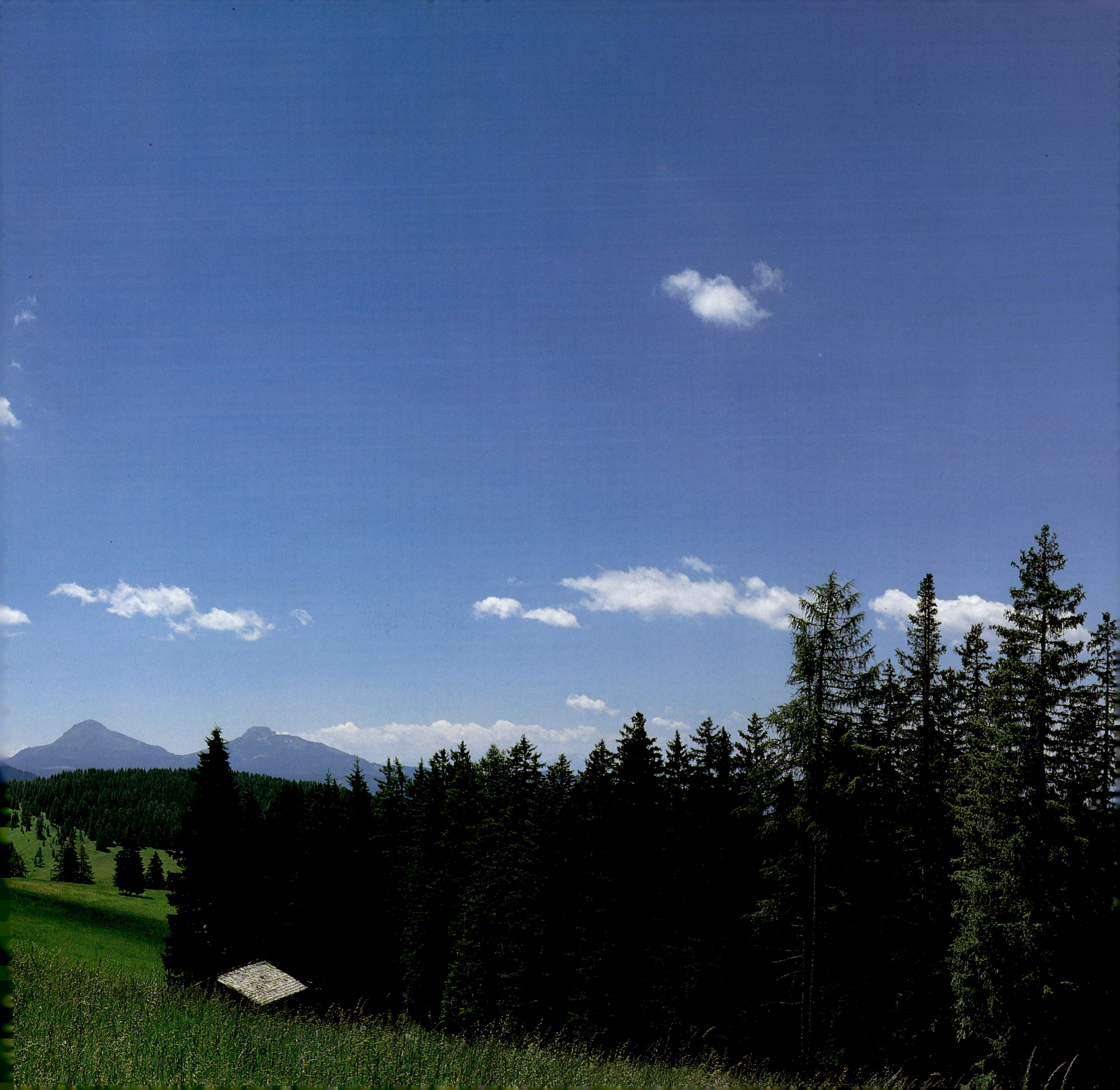

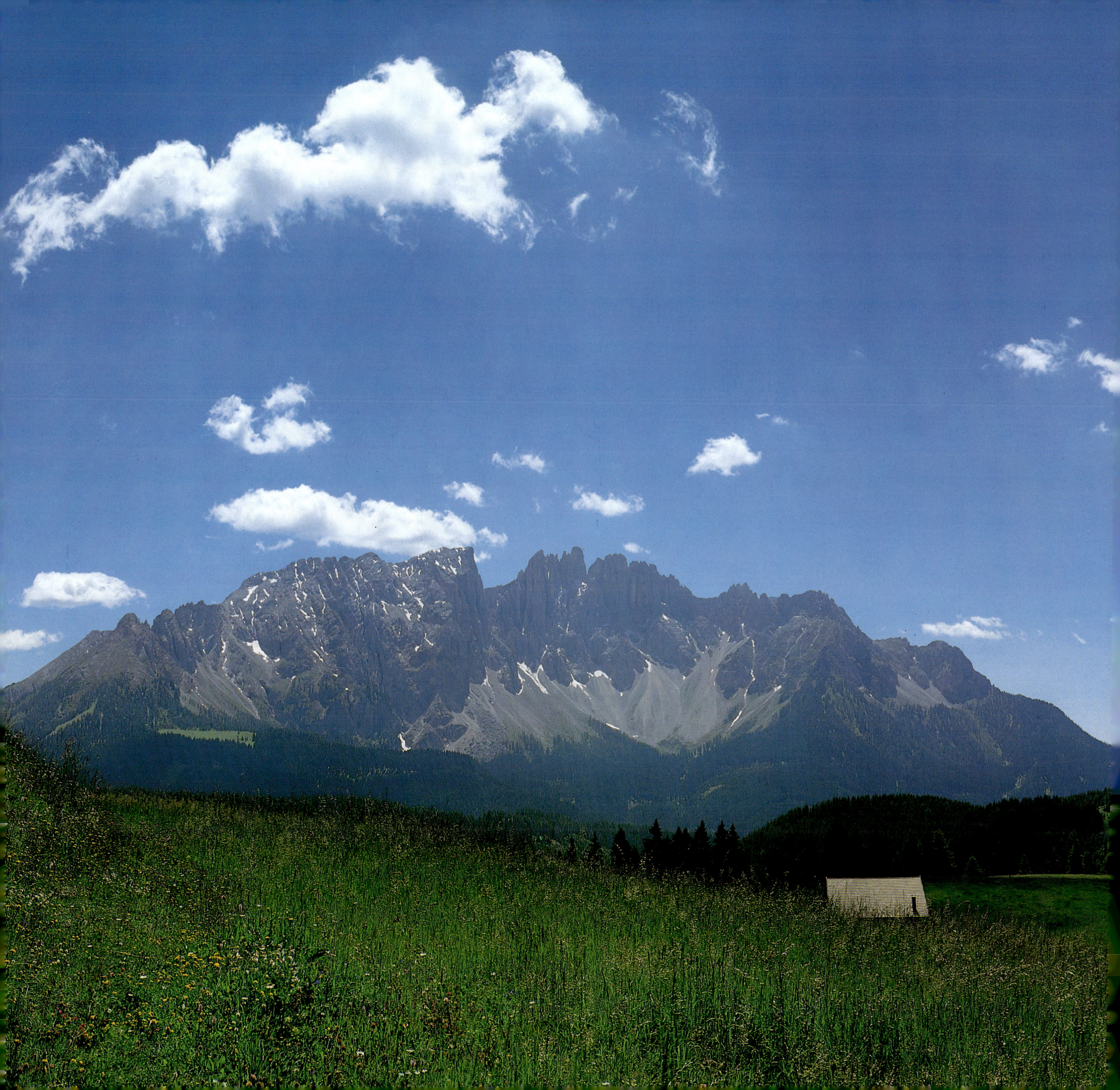

20\. Tierser Tal mit den Vajolettürmen.
Val di Tires. Torri del Vaiolèt.
Долина Тирес. Башни местечка Вайолет.
ティーレス谷。　　トーリ・デル・ヴァイオレットゥ

21\. Rotwand.
Roda di Vaèl.
Рода ди Вайел.
ローダ・ディ・ヴァエル

22\. Blick von der Zannser-Alm auf die Geislerspitzen.
Malga Zànnes. Le Odle.
Пастушья хижина Дзаннес. Ле Одле.
ザンネス放牧小屋。　　オードゥレ

23\. Peitlerkofel über dem Würzjoch.
Passo delle Erbe. Sass de Pútia.
Псревал Эрбе. Сасс де Путия.
エルベ峠。　　サッス・ディ・プーティア

24\. Schindeldach.
Scandole.
Скандолэ.
スカンドレ（こけら葺き）

21.

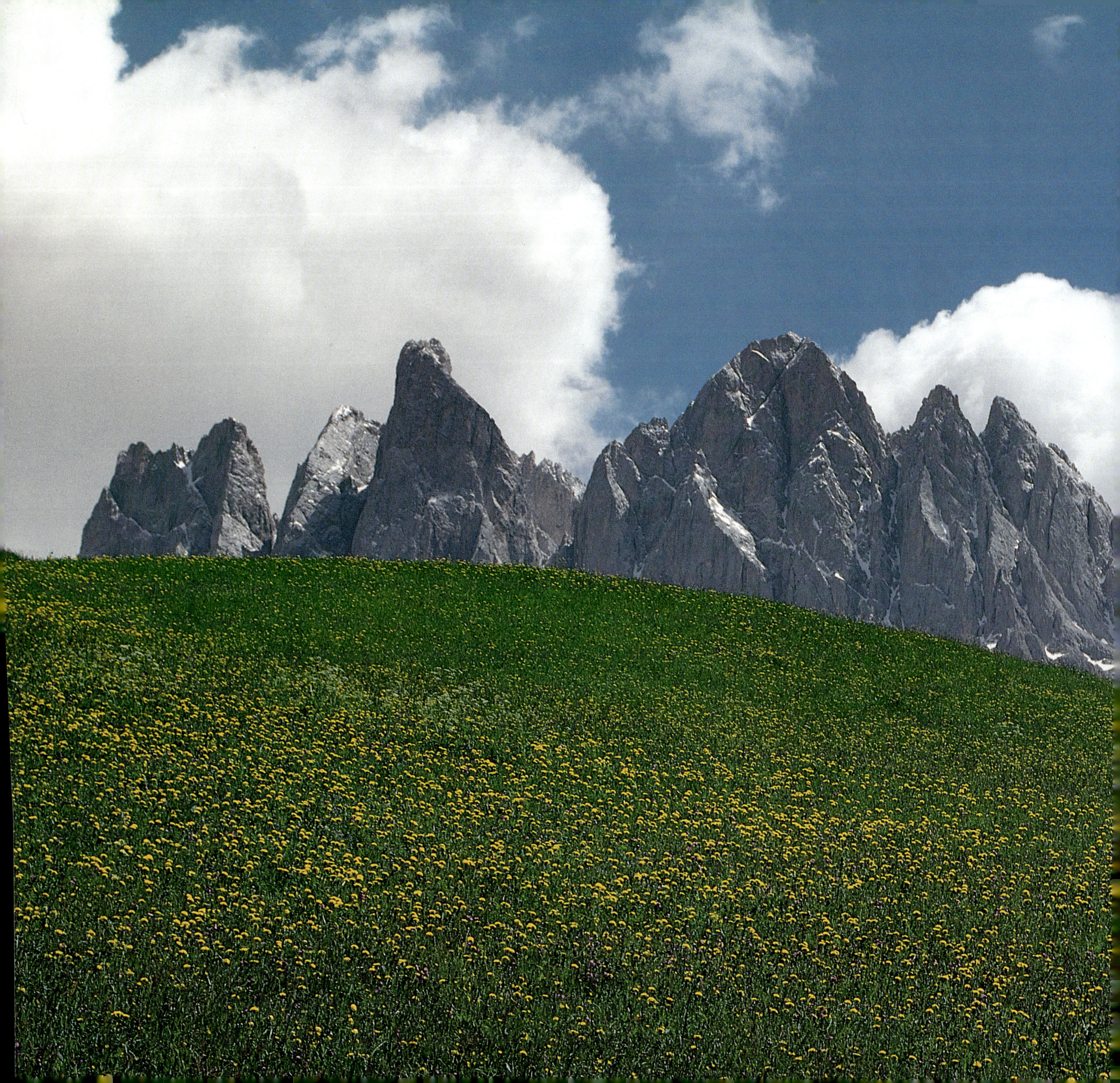

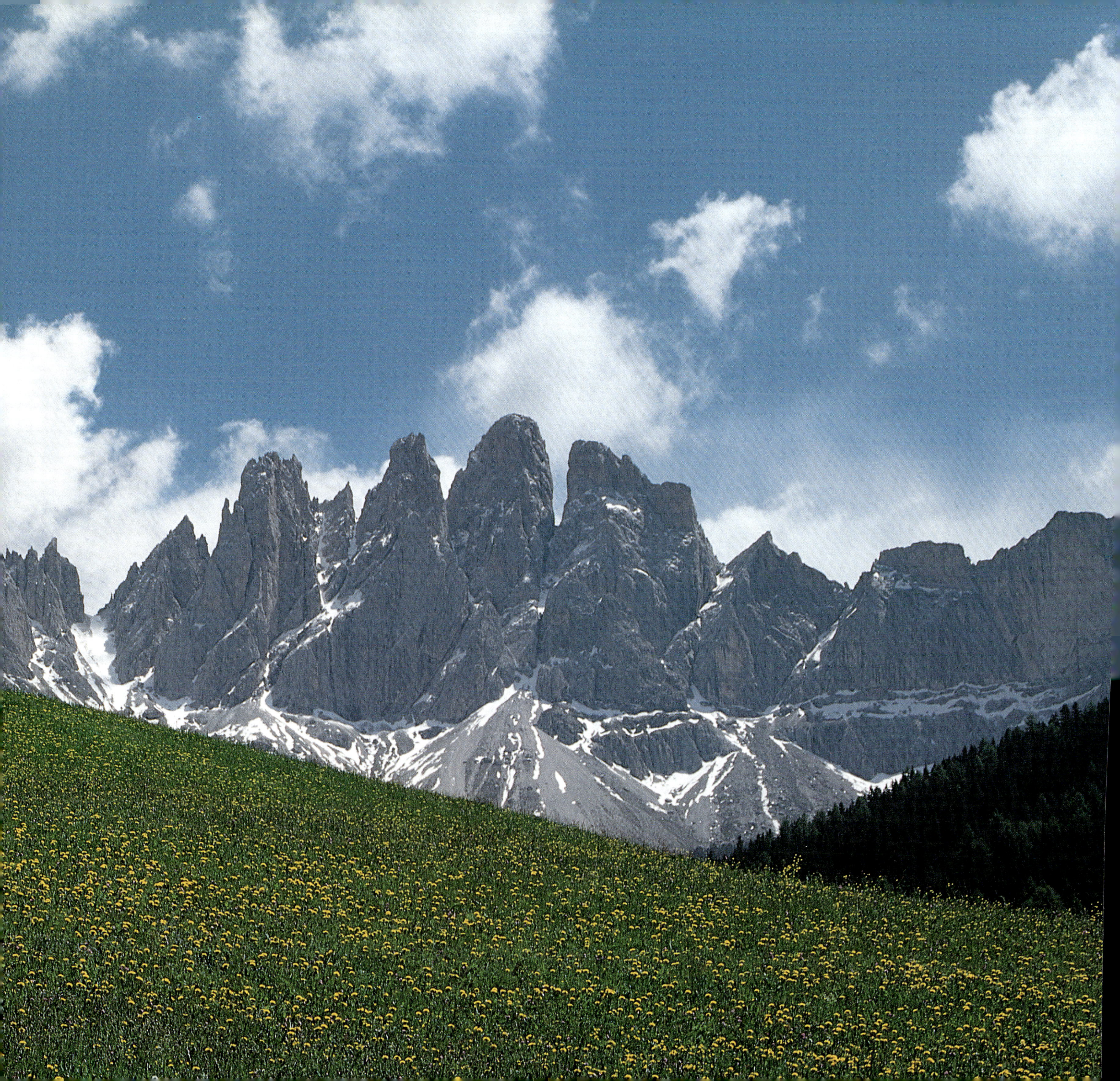

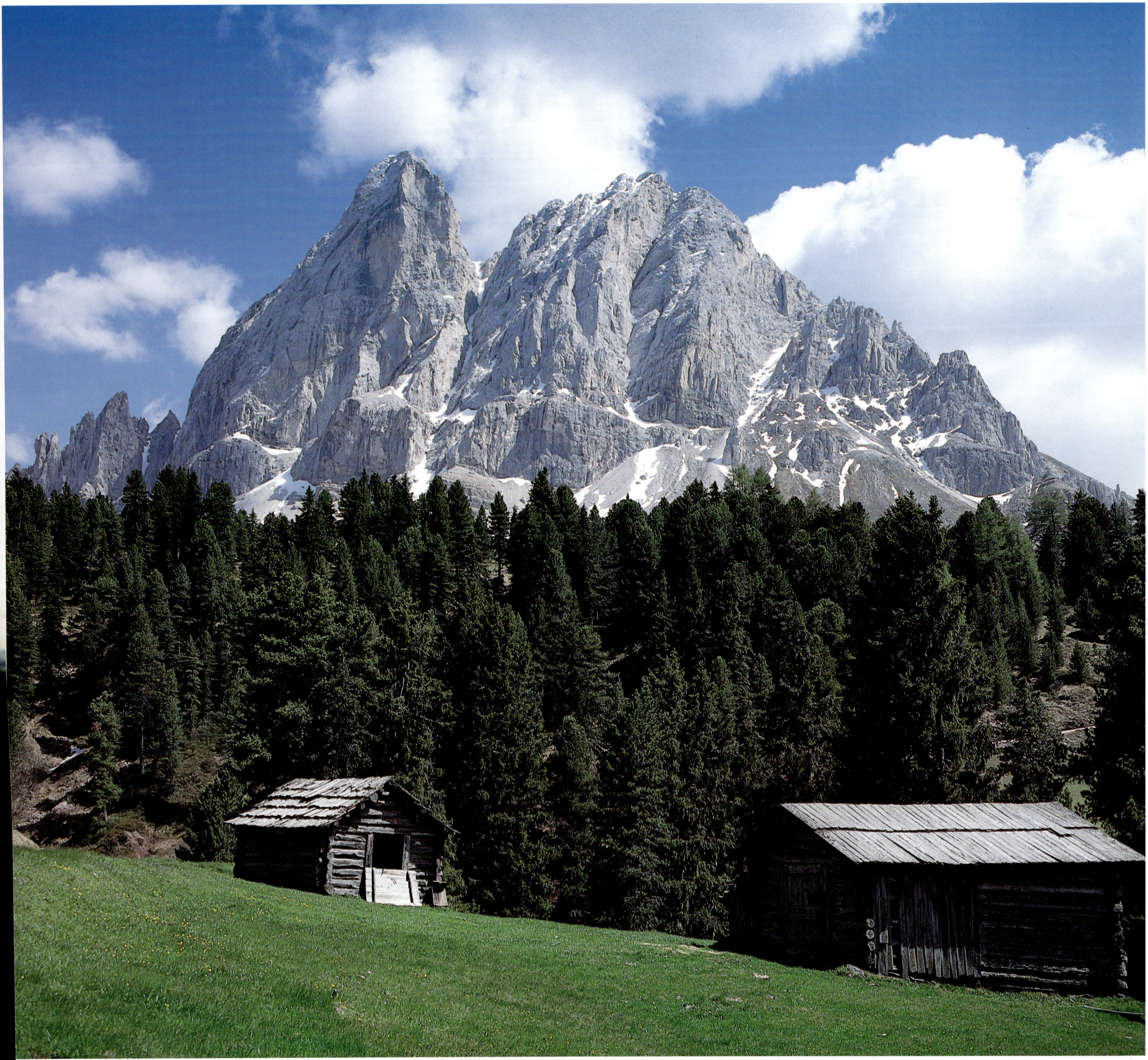

24.

25. Cortina d'Ampezzo.
Кортина д'Ампеццо.
コルティーナ・ダンベッツォ

26. Tofana di Rozes.
Тофана ди Розц.
トォファーナ・ディ・ローゼス

27. Am Giau-Paß.
Passo Giau.
Перевал Чиау.
ジィアウ峠

28. Rundblick auf das Becken von Ampezzo.
La conca ampezzana in una panoramica a 360°.
A 360° panorama of the Ampezzo cirque.
Le bassin d'Ampezzo en une vue panoramique à 360°.
La cuenca de Ampezzo en una panorámica de 360°.
Котловина Ампеццана, панорамный вид на 360°.
アンベッツォ盆地を360°パノラマ写真で見る

29. Cinque Torri in den Ampezzaner Dolomiten.
30. *Dolomiti ampezzane. Cinque Torri.*
The Ampezzo Dolomites. The Cinque Torri.
Dolomites d'Ampezzo. Cinque Torri.
Dolomitas de Ampezzo. Cinco Torres.
Доломиты Ампеццанэ. Пять Башен.
ドロミーティ・アンベッツァーネ。
チンクゥエ・トーリ

31. Fanes-Alpe.
Alpe di Fànes.
Альпы Фаннс.
アルペ・ディ・ファンネス

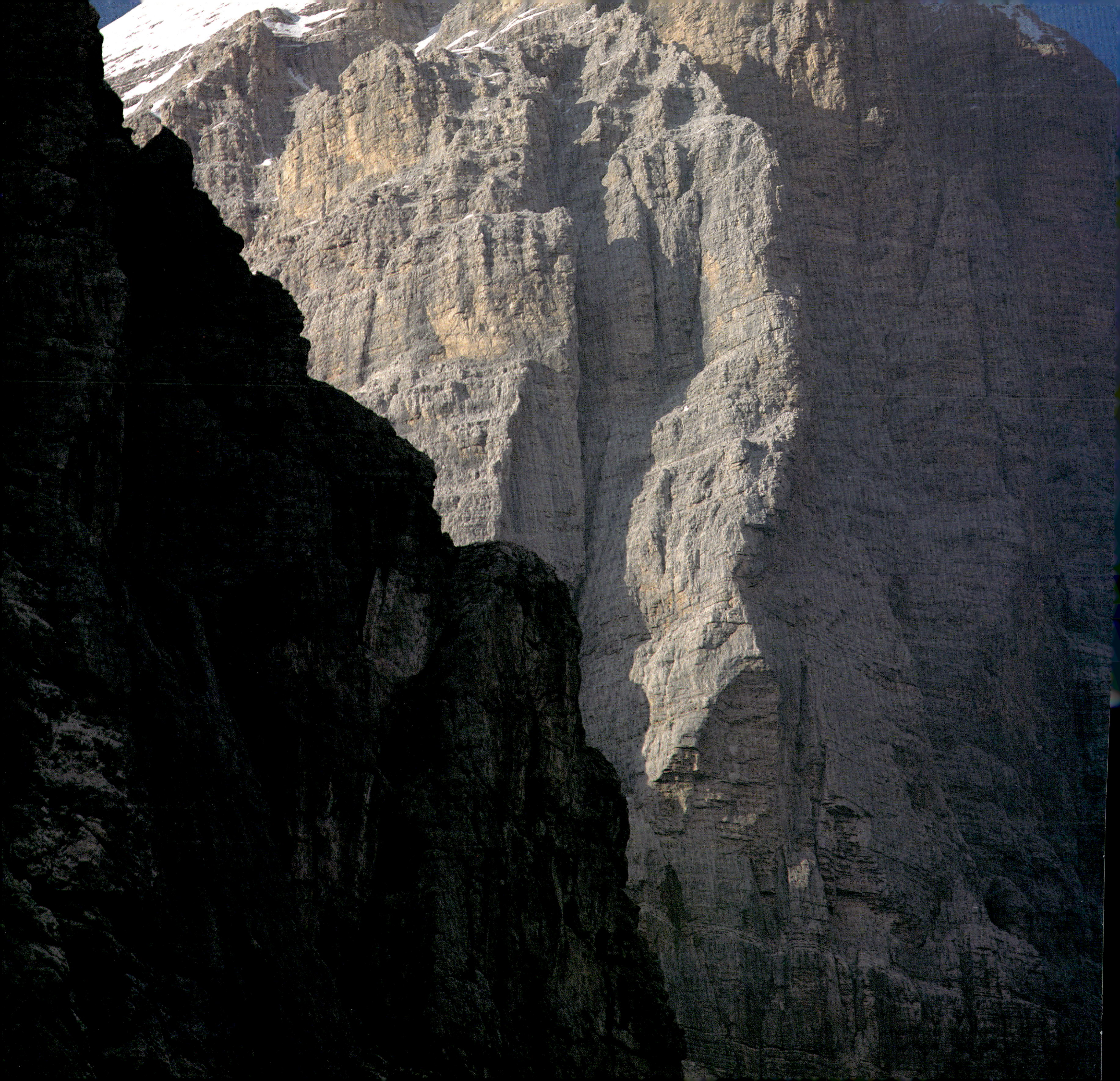

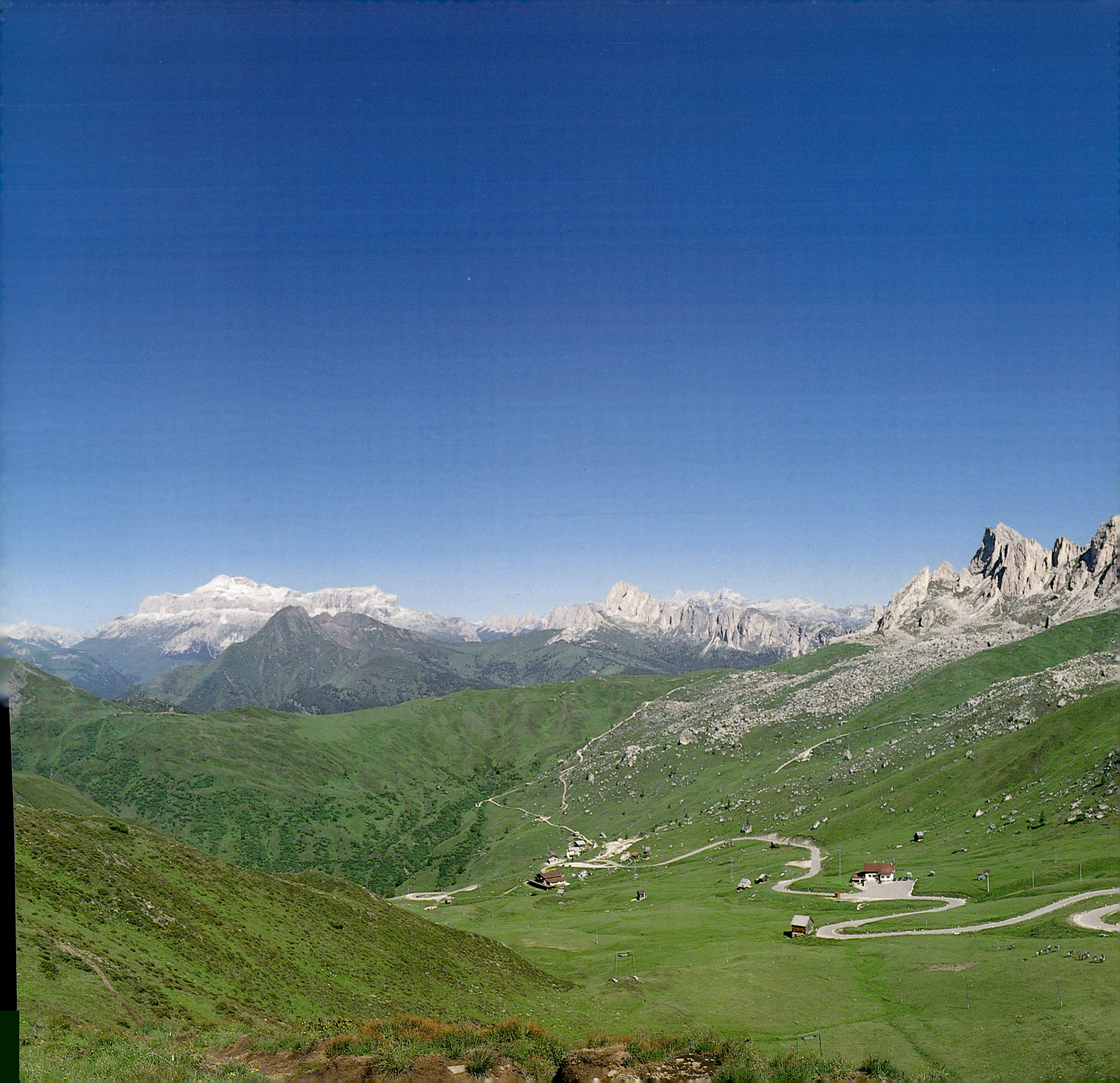

Flora

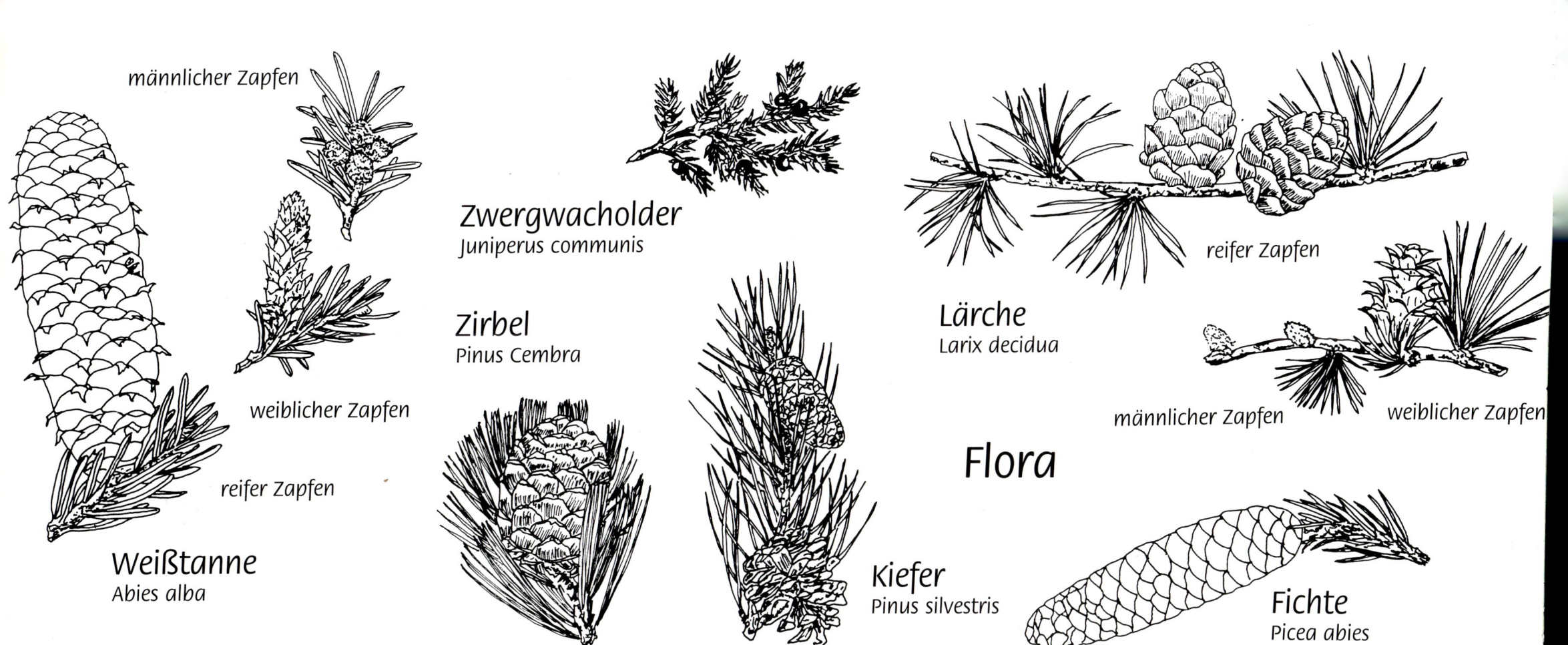

Weißtanne
Abies alba
- männlicher Zapfen
- weiblicher Zapfen
- reifer Zapfen

Zirbel
Pinus Cembra

Zwergwacholder
Juniperus communis

Kiefer
Pinus silvestris

Lärche
Larix decidua
- reifer Zapfen
- männlicher Zapfen
- weiblicher Zapfen

Fichte
Picea abies

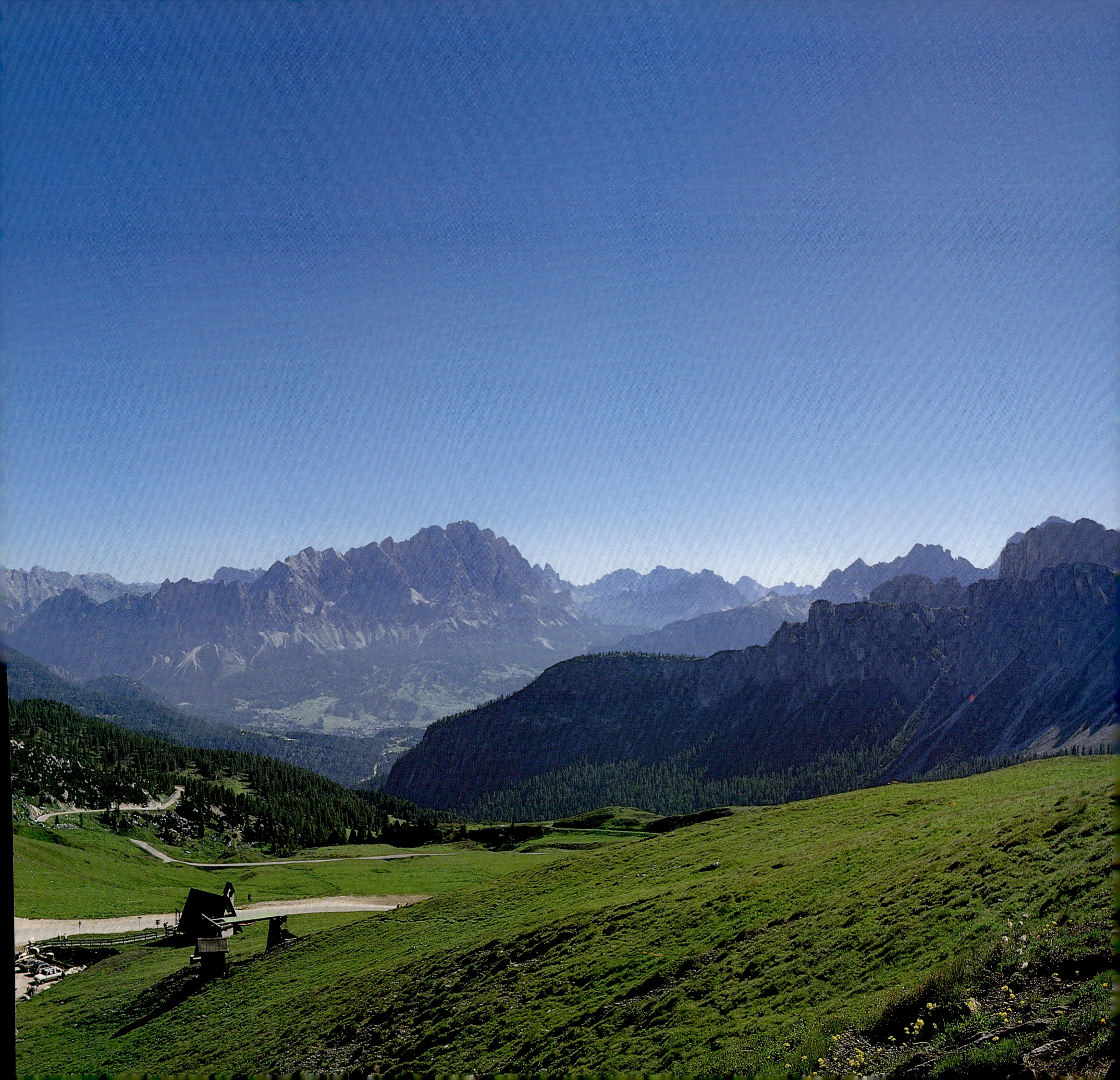

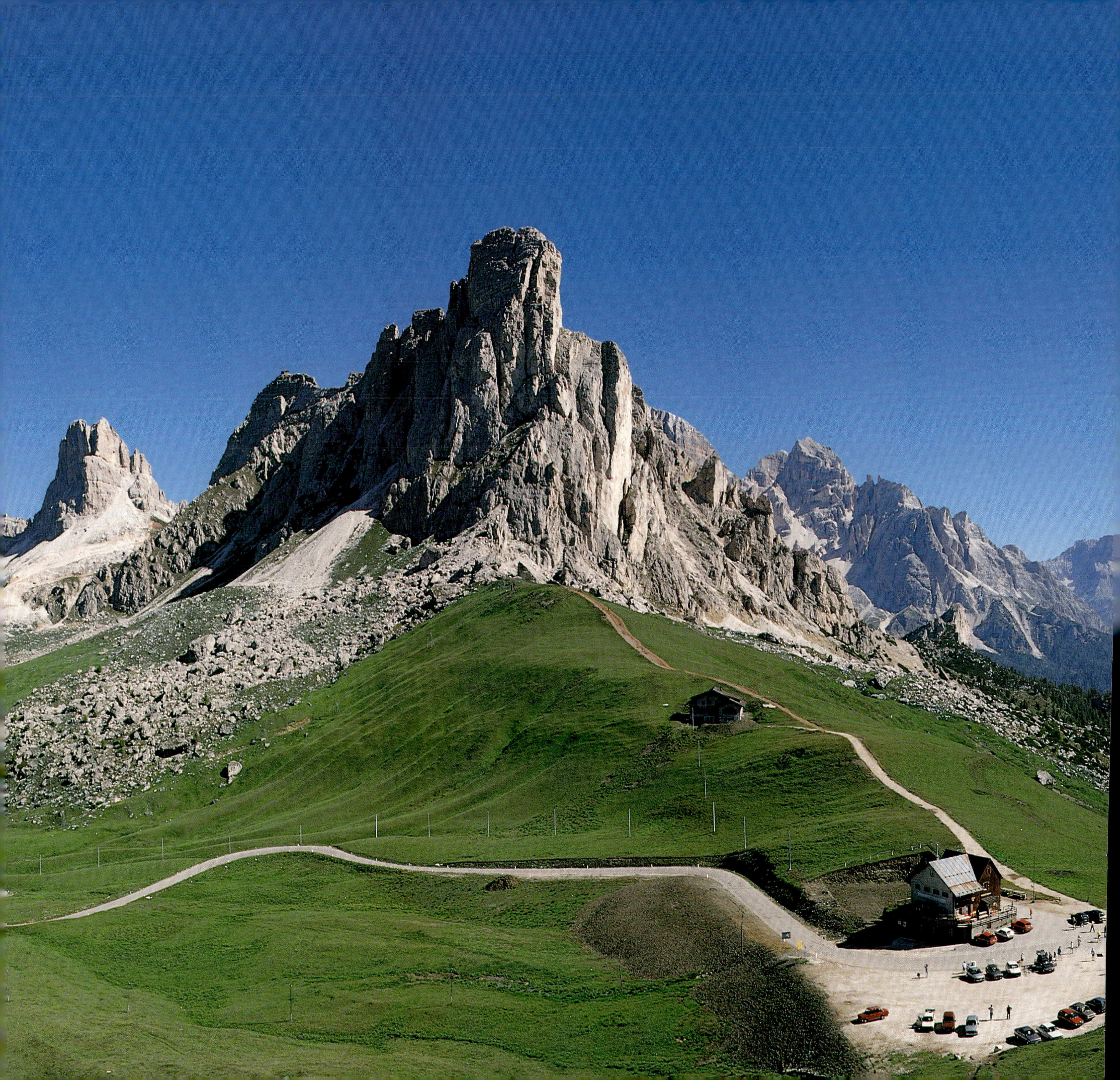

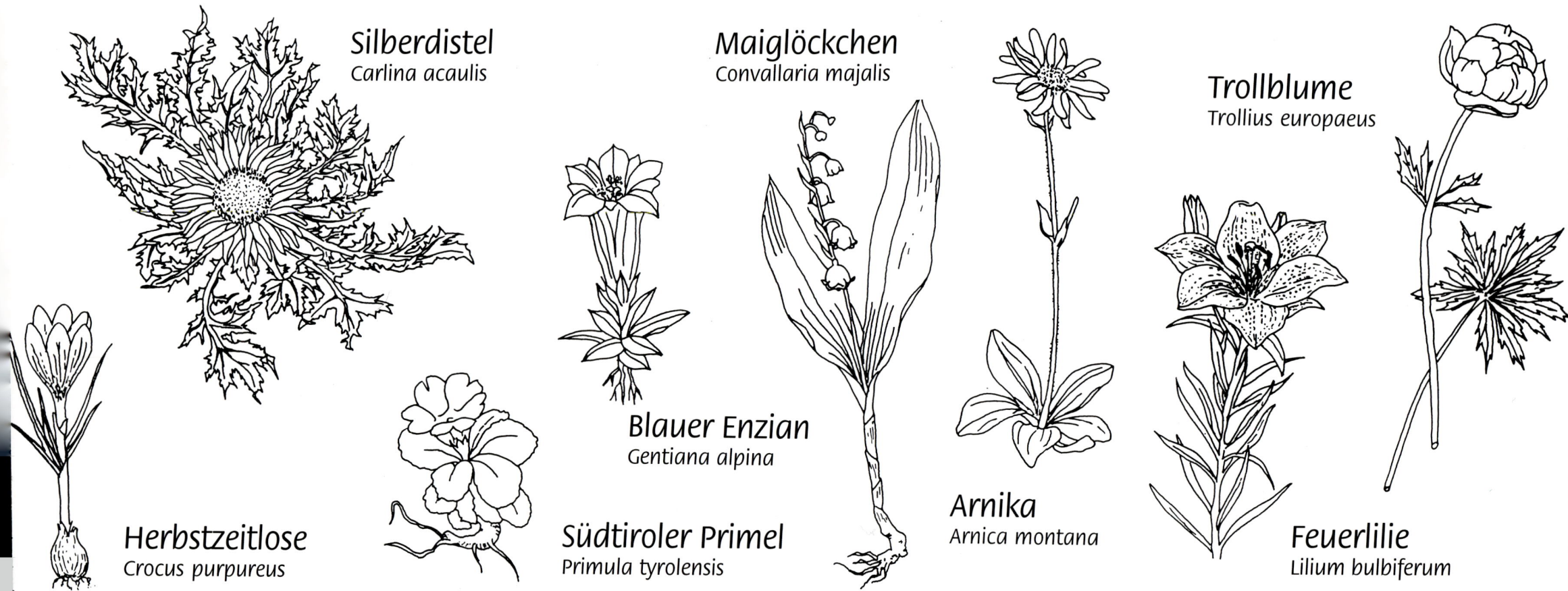

Silberdistel
Carlina acaulis

Maiglöckchen
Convallaria majalis

Trollblume
Trollius europaeus

Herbstzeitlose
Crocus purpureus

Blauer Enzian
Gentiana alpina

Südtiroler Primel
Primula tyrolensis

Arnika
Arnica montana

Feuerlilie
Lilium bulbiferum

Edelweiß
Leontopodium alpinum

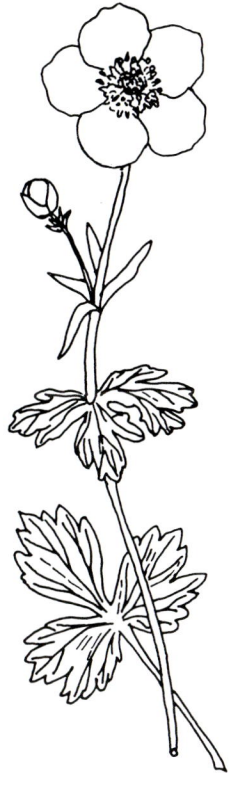

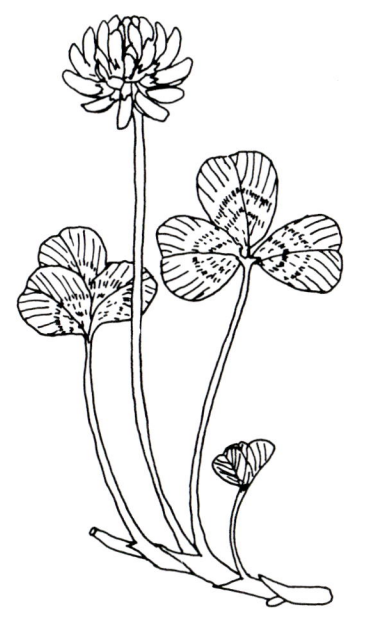

Weißer Klee
Trifolium repens

Alpenrose
Rhododendron ferragineum

Himbeeren
Rubus Idaeus

Berghahnenfuß
Ranunculus montanus

Schwarzes Kohlröschen
Nequitella nigra

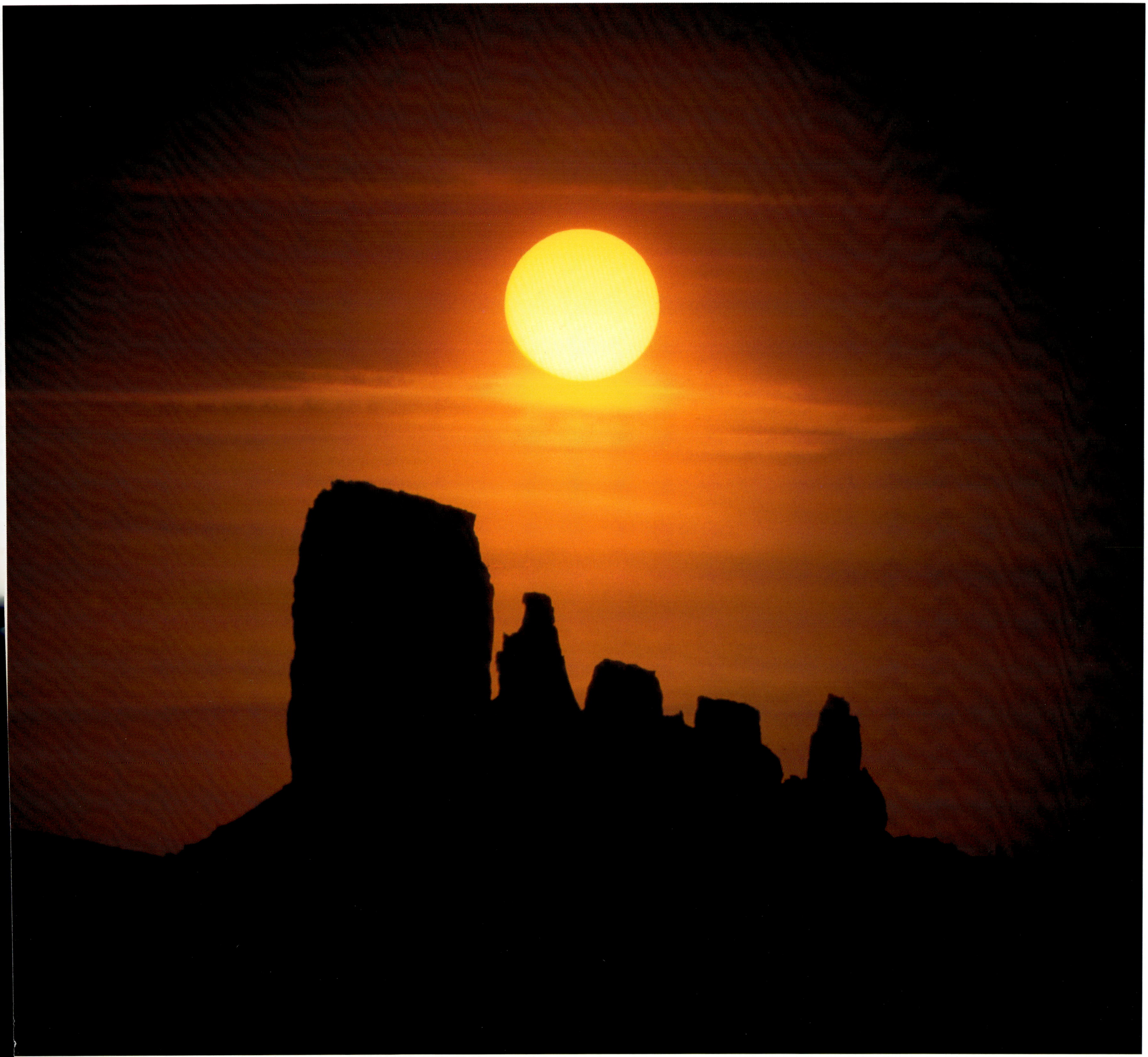

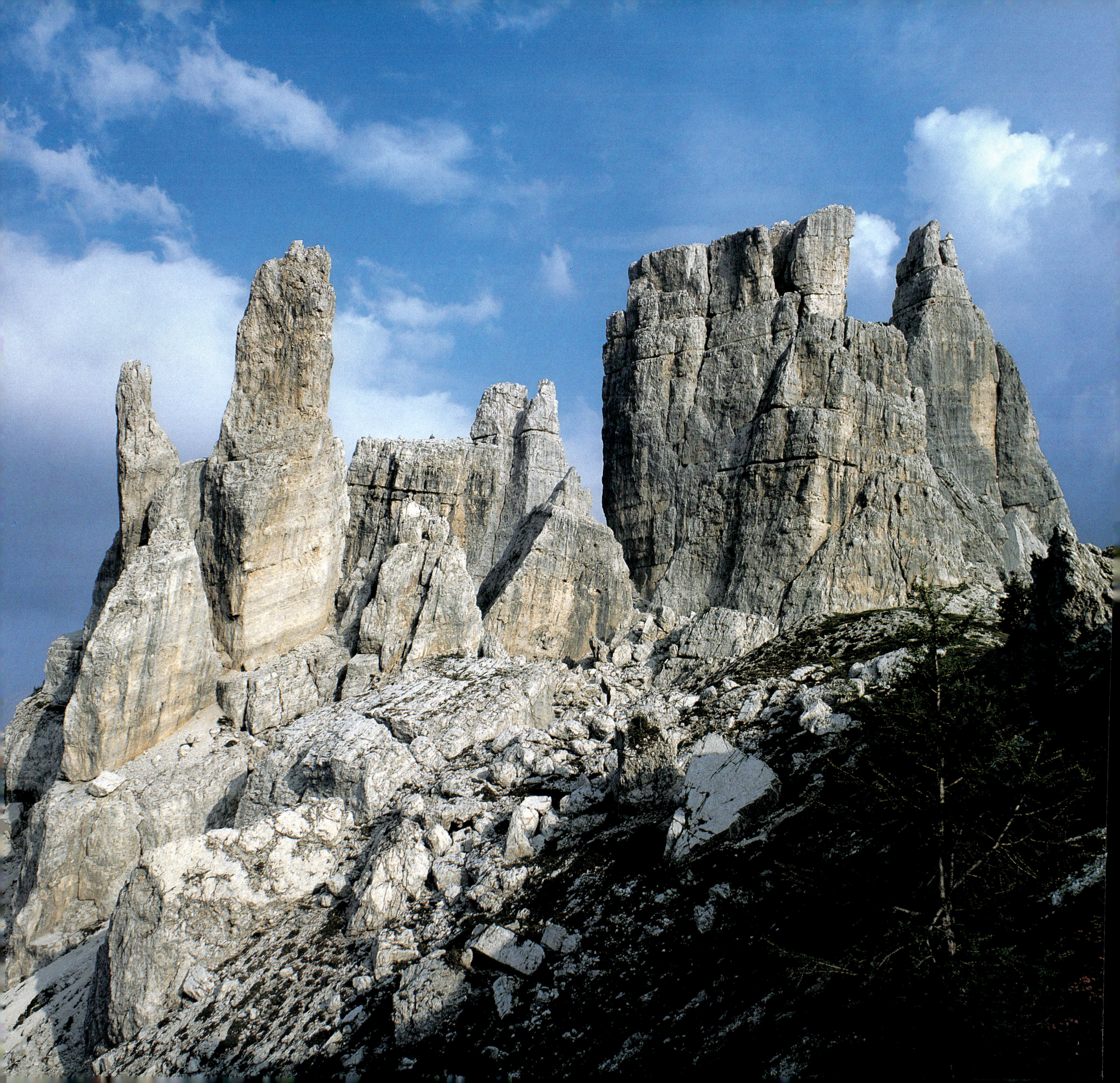

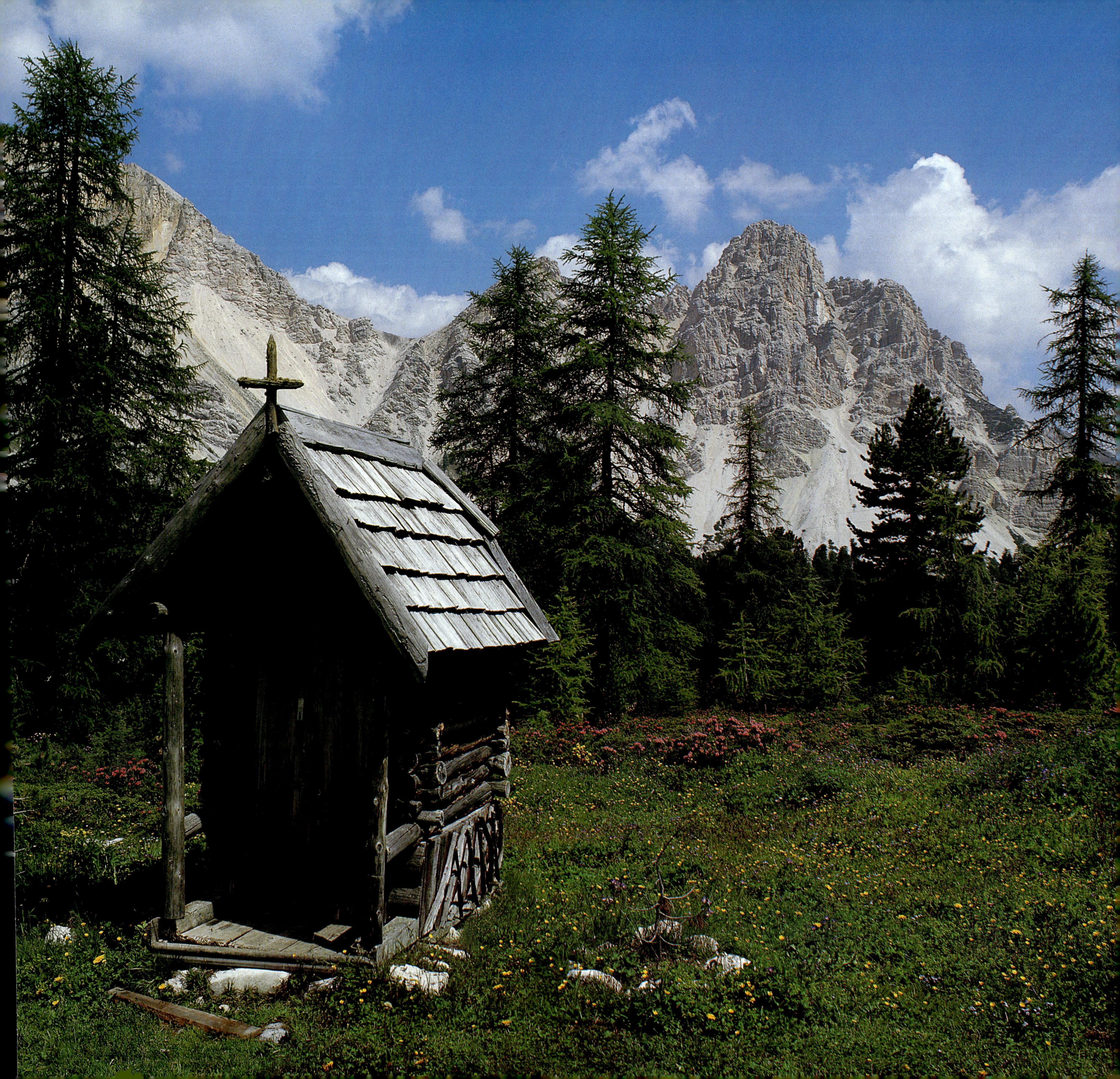

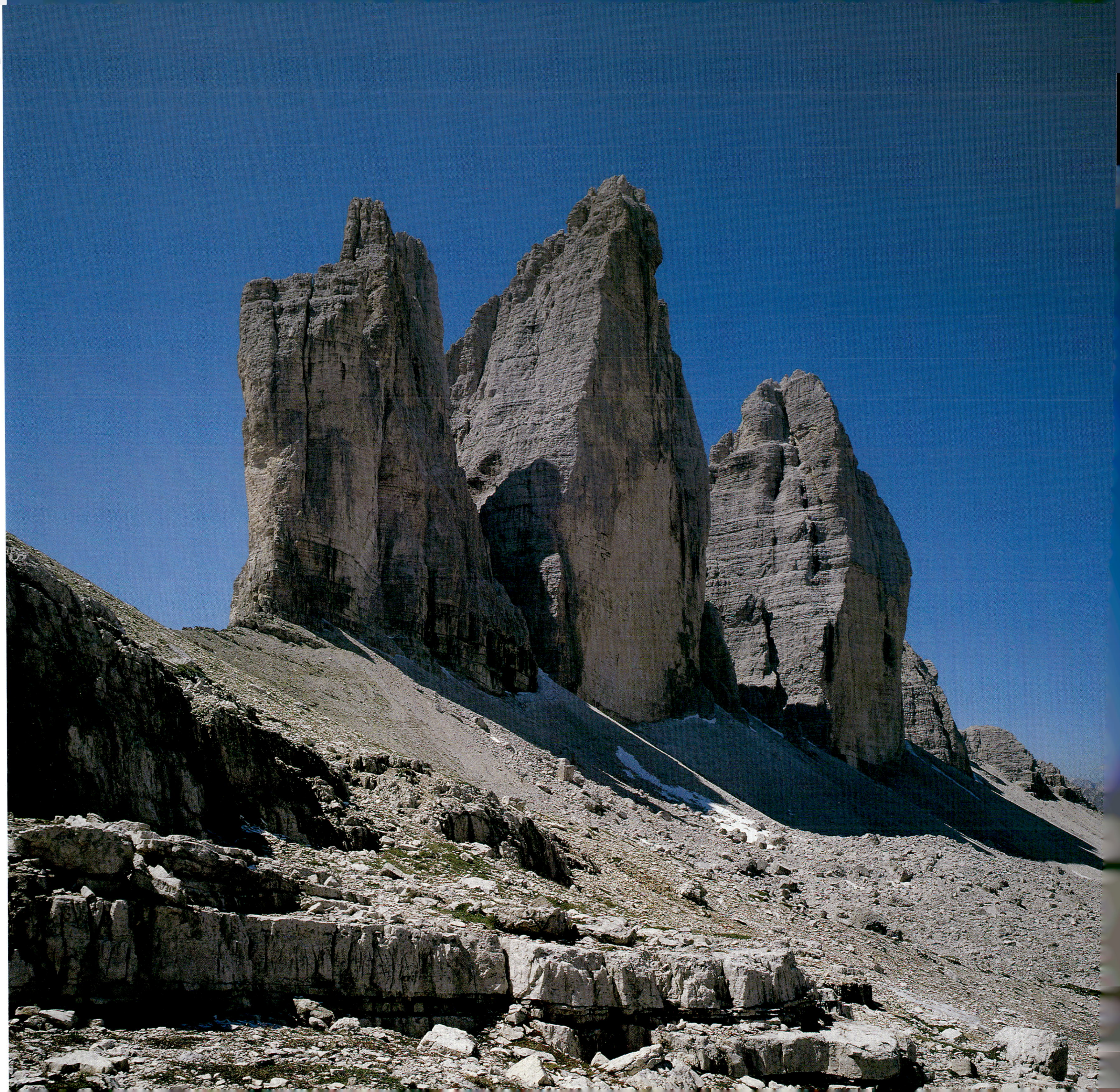

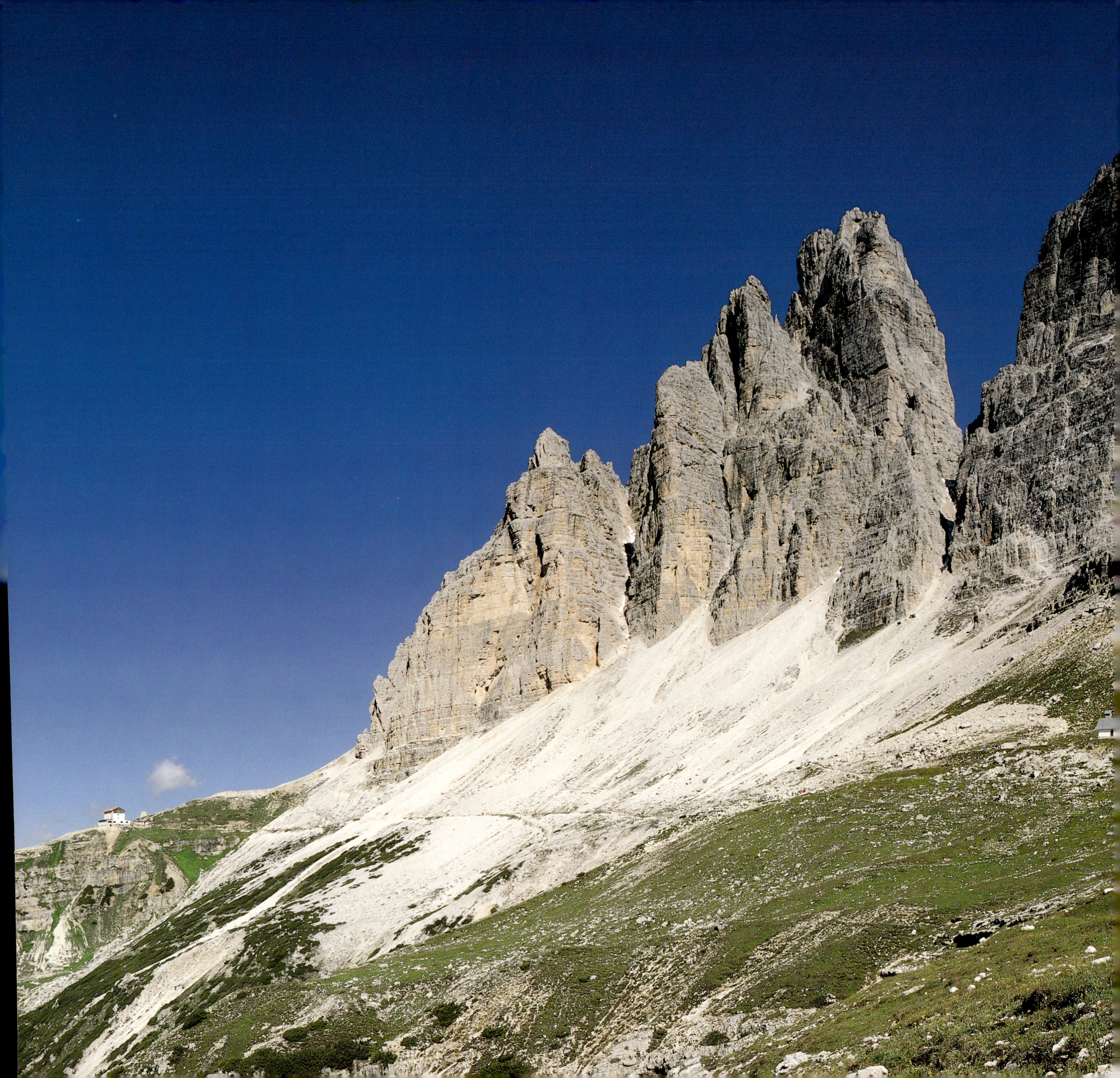

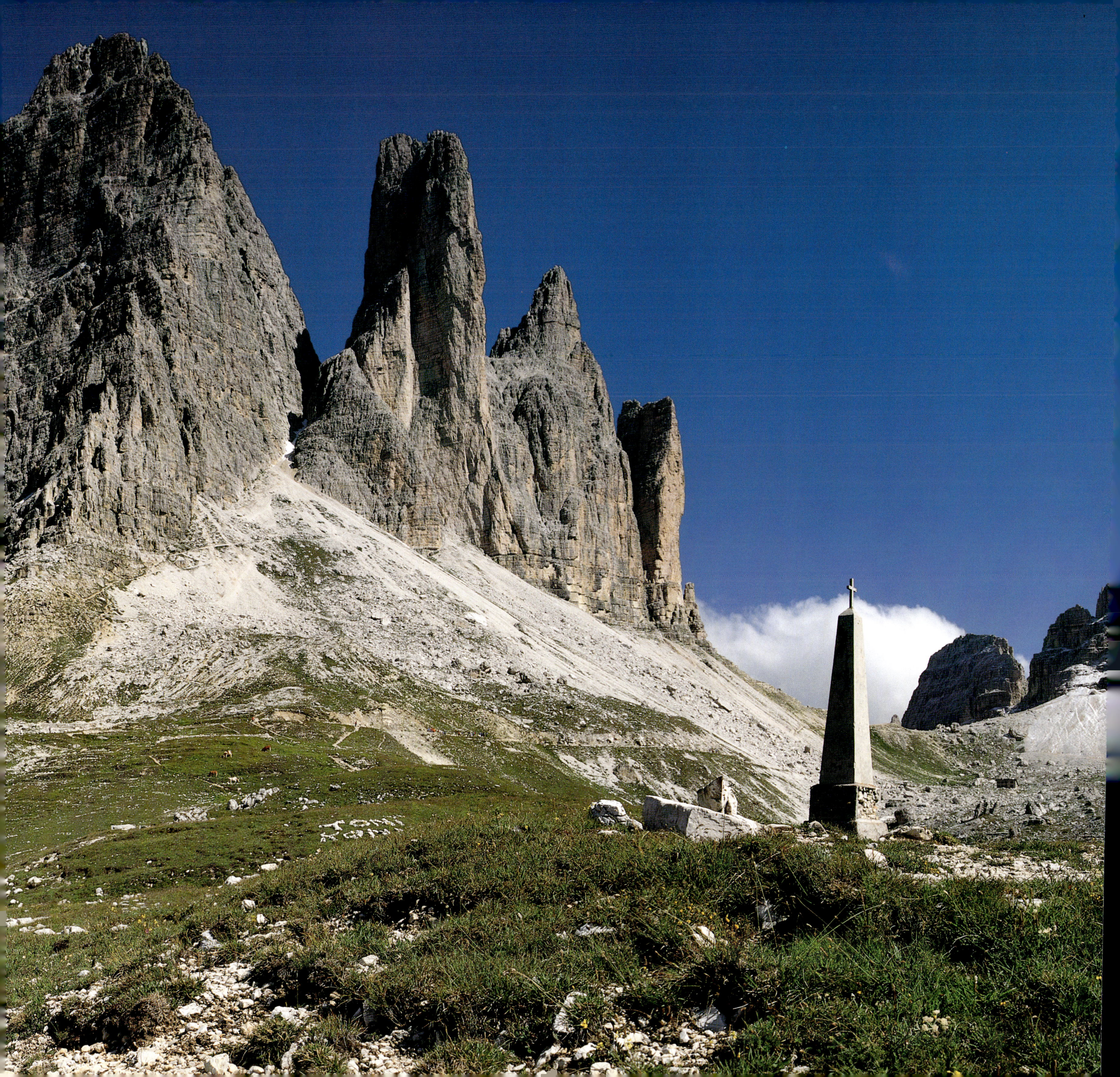

Die Spuren der Tiere

Dachs
Meles meles

Fuchs
Vulpes vulpes

Hase
Lepus europaeus

Wiesel
Mustela nivalis

Eichhörnchen
Sciurus vulgaris

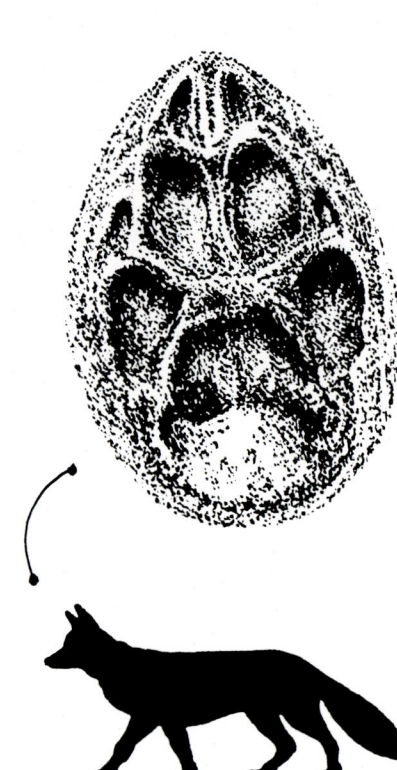

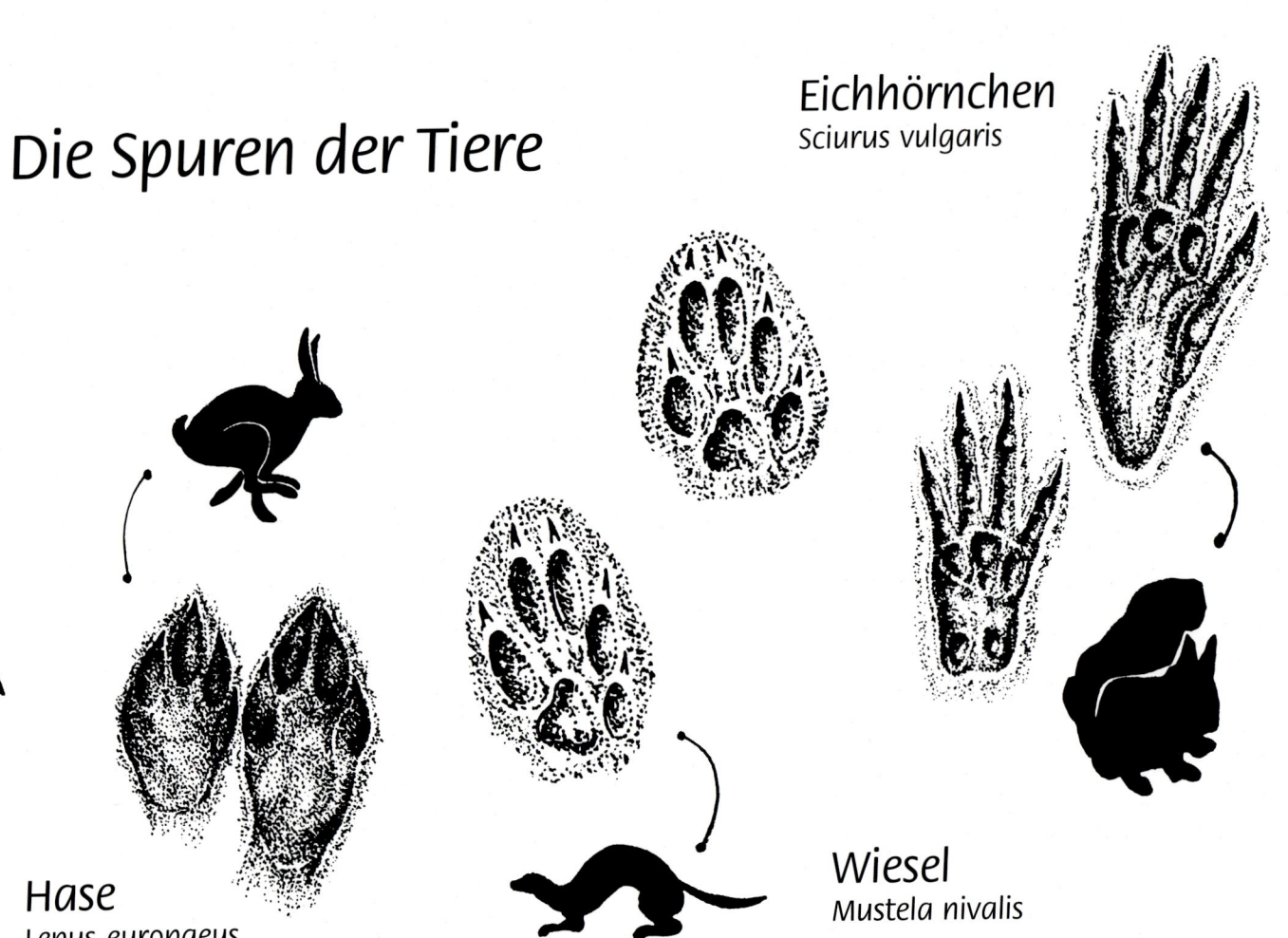

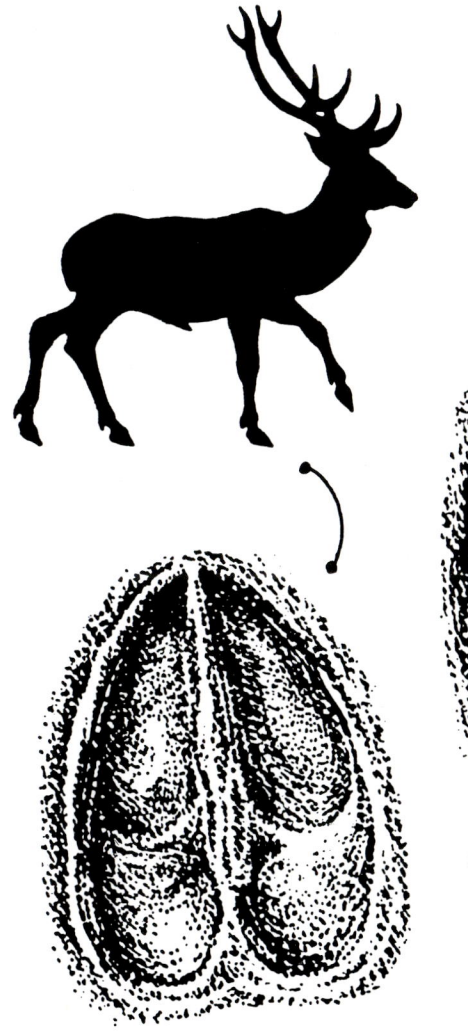

Hirsch
Cervus elaphus

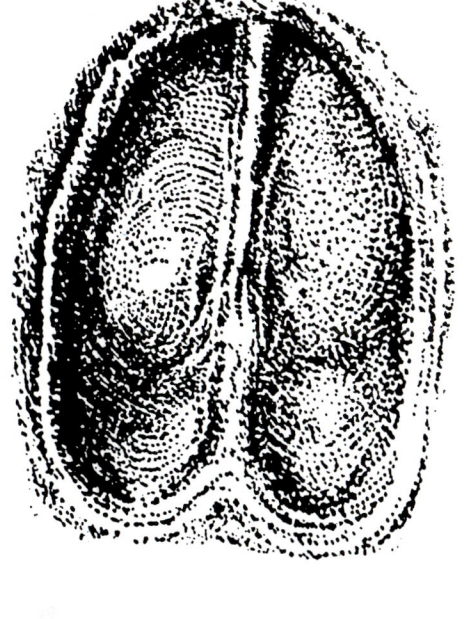

Reh
Capreolus capreolus

Gemse
Rupicapra rupicapra

32. Die Nordwände der Drei Zinnen.
Cime di Lavaredo. Le celebri pareti nord.
The Cime di Lavaredo. The renowned North faces.
Sommets de Lavaredo. Les célèbres parois nord.
Cimas de Lavaredo. Las célebres paredes norte.
Вершины Лаваредо. Знаменитые северные стены.
チーマ・ディ・ラヴァレード。　その名も高い北壁

33. Drei Zinnen.
Cime di Lavaredo.
Вершины Лаваредо.
チーマ・ディ・ラヴァレード

34. Segantini-Hütte mit Pala-Gruppe.
Baita Segantini. Pale di San Martino.
Горное убежище Сегантини и Столбы Сан Мартино.
セガンティーニ小屋とサン・マルティーノ岩峰

35. Venegia-Tal mit Pala-Gruppe.
Val Venègia. Pale di San Martino.
Долина Венеджия. Столбы Сан Мартино.
ヴェネージィア谷。　サン・マルティーノ岩峰

36. Cimòn della Pala.
Чимон делла Пала.
チモン・デッラ・パーラ

36.

37. Pfarrkirche von Transacqua im Primiero.
Primiero. Pieve di Transacqua.
Primiero. The Transacqua parish church.
Primiero. Eglise de Transacqua.
Primiero. Iglesia de Transacqua.
Примиеро. Церквушка Транзаквуа.
プリミエーロ村。
ピエーヴェ・デイ・トランザクワ

38. Physoplexis comosa.
Физоплексис комоза.
フィーソプレックスィス・コモーザ

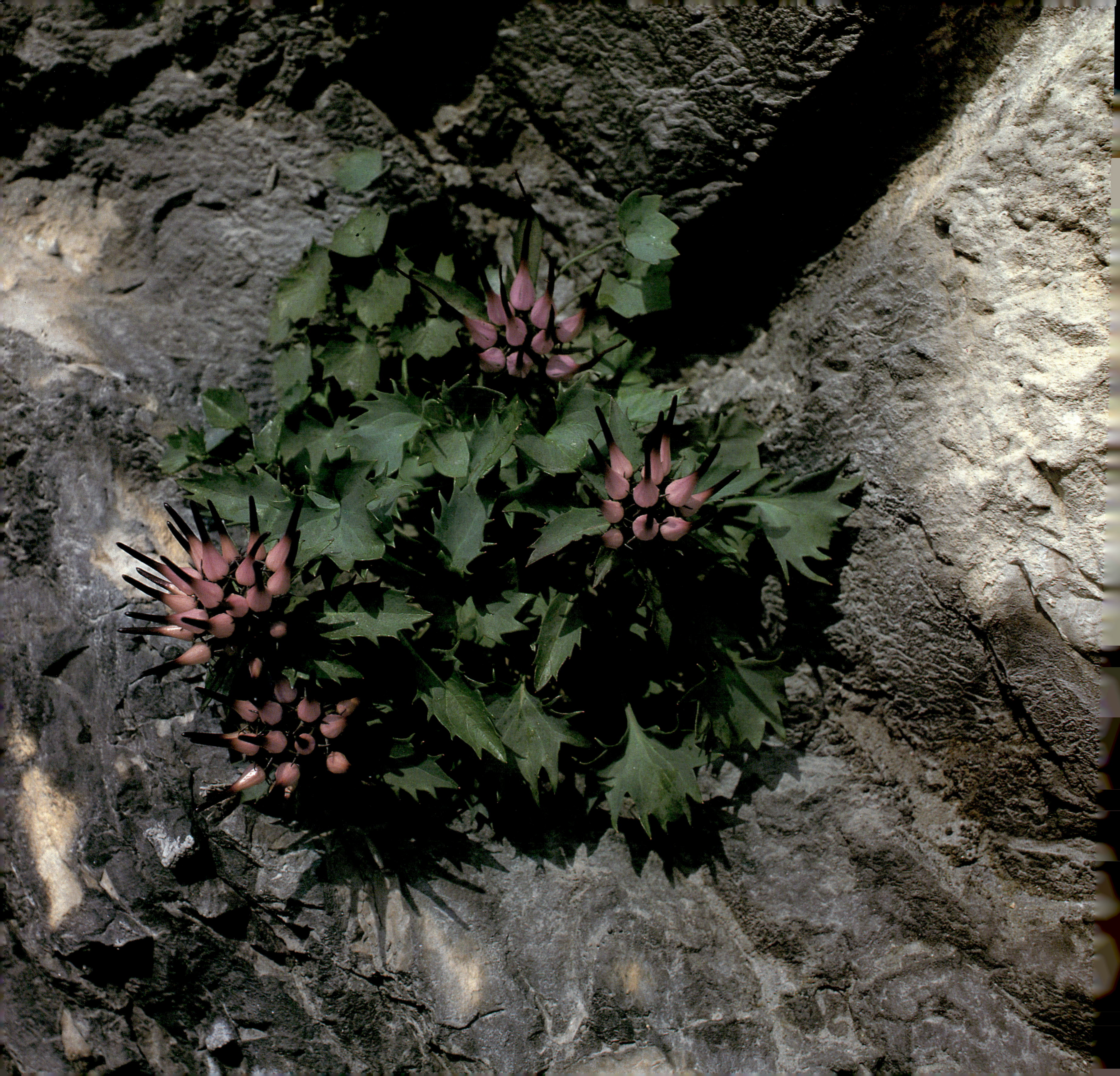

40.

Kloster Neustift
bei Brixen

befestigte Kapelle

Grundriß des
Erdgeschosses

Schloß Tirol
im Etschtal

Haupt
der Ka

Grundriß

St. Martin
im Abteital

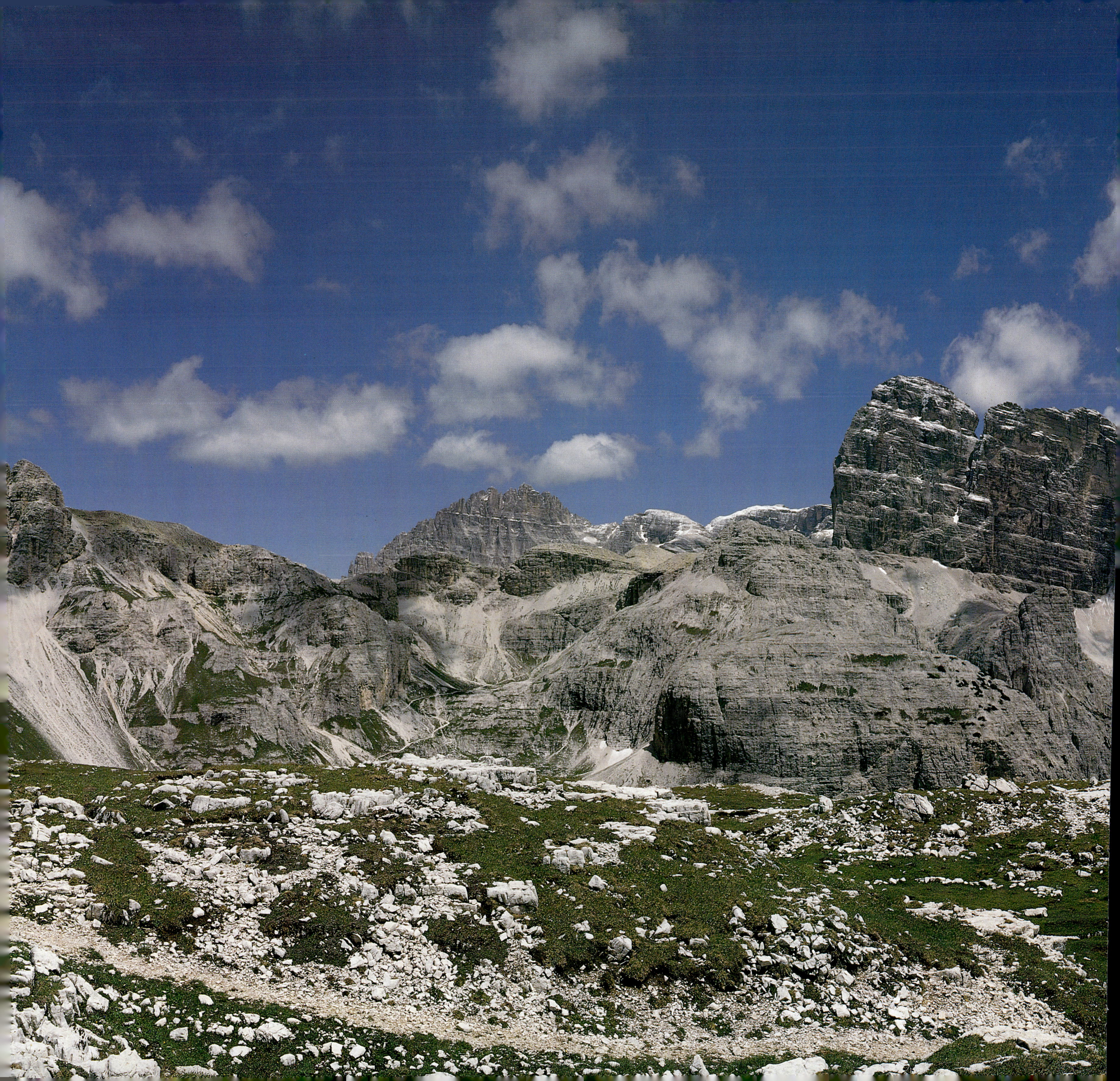

Stenico, 8. Jahrhundert, Detail

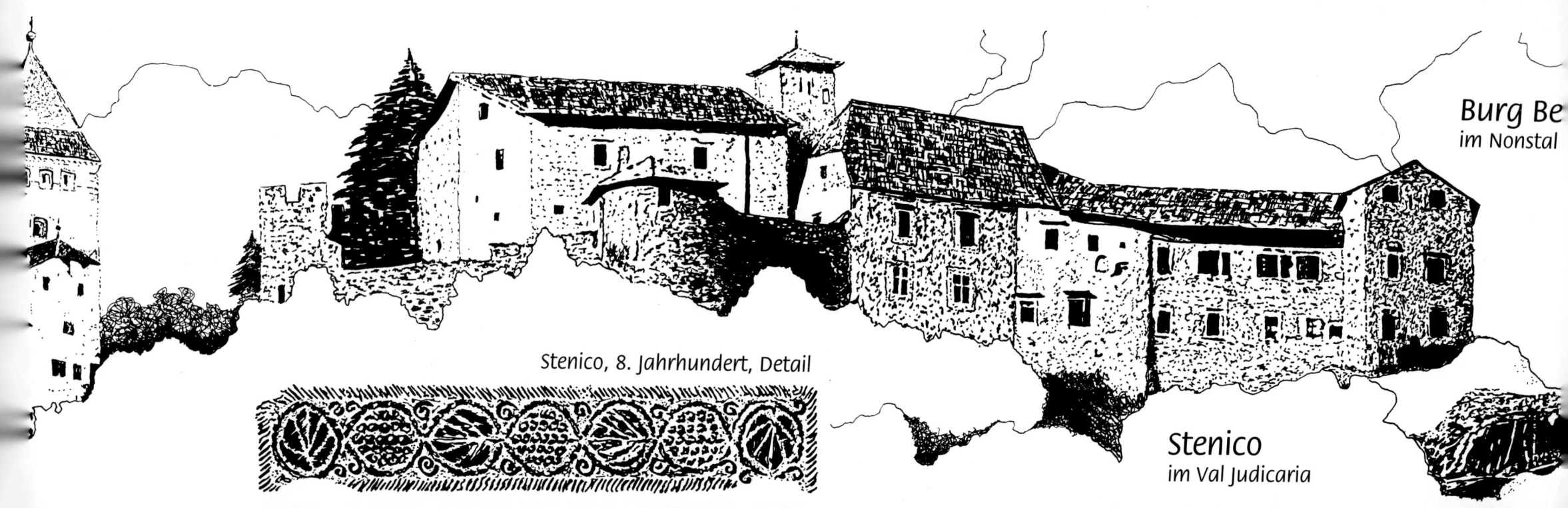

Burg Be
im Nonstal

Stenico
im Val Judicaria

Burg Ossana
im Valle di Sole

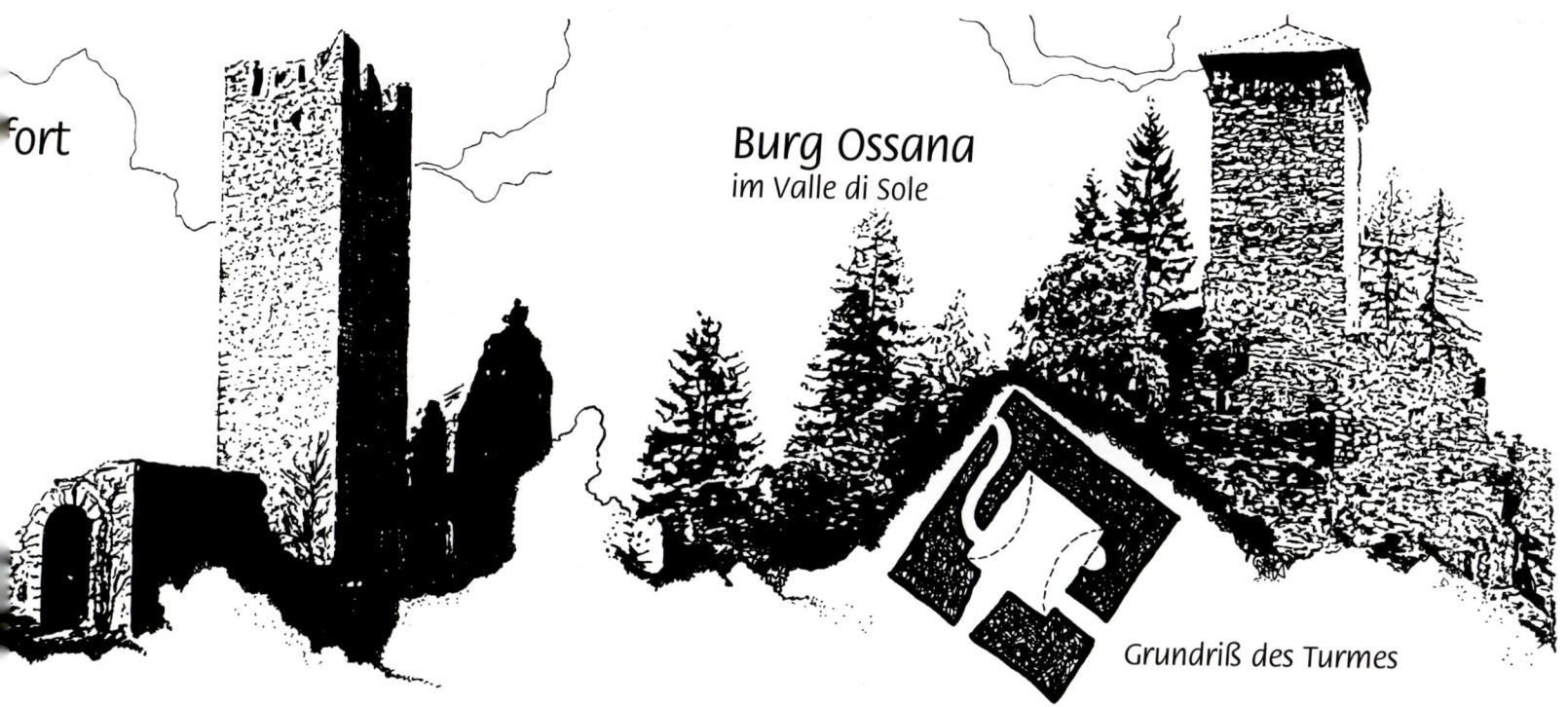

Grundriß des Turmes

39. Marmolata. Rundblick von der Punta Rocca.
Marmolada. Panorama a 360° dalla Punta Rocca.
Marmolada. A 360° panorama from the Punta Rocca.
Marmolada. Panorama à 360° de la Punta Rocca.
Marmolada. Panorama de 360° desde la Punta Rocca.
Мармолада. Панорамный вид на 360° Вершины Рокка.
マルモラーダ。プンタ・デ・ロッカからの360°パノラマ写真

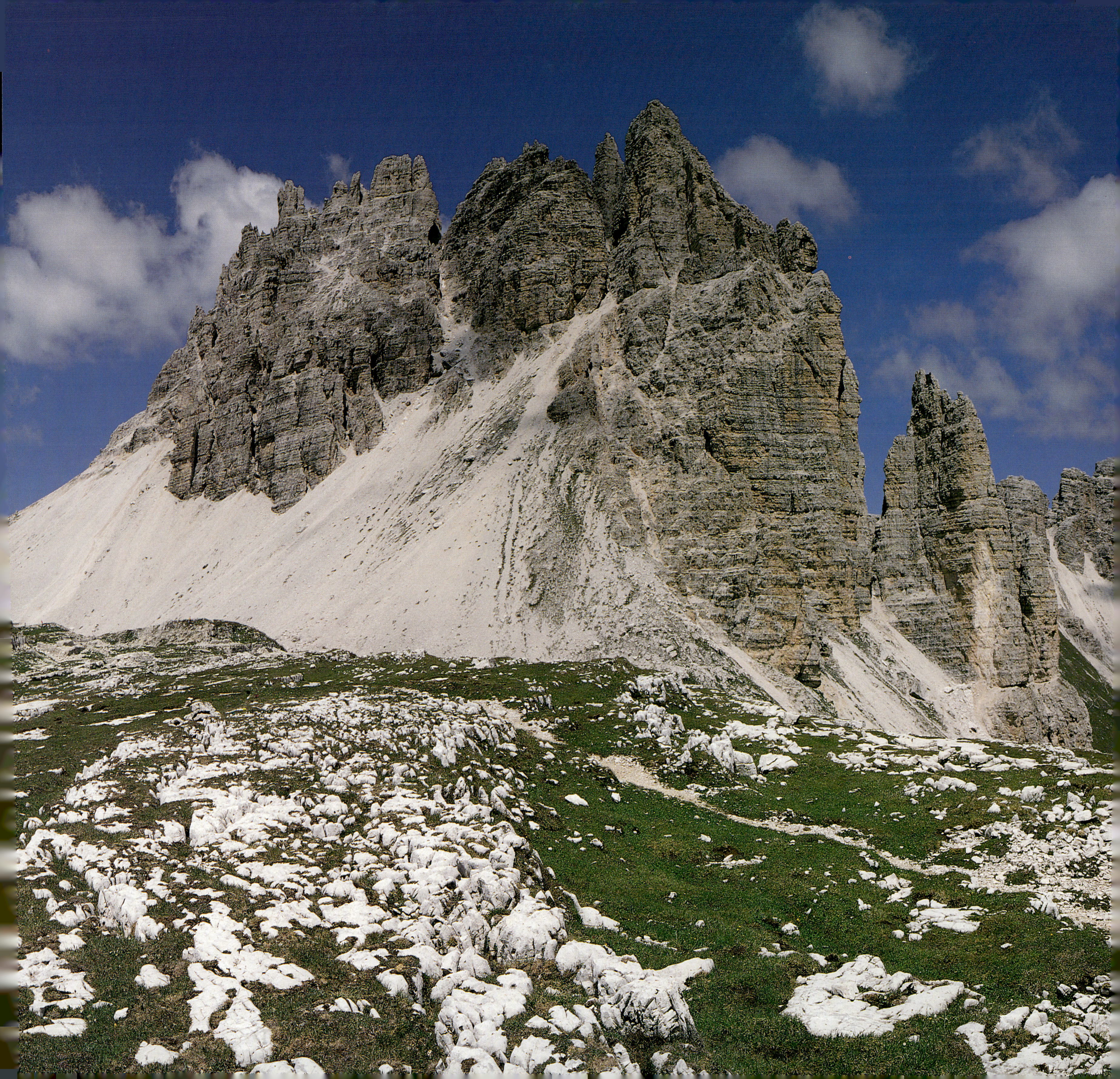

Burgen in den Tälern der Dolomiten

Burg Maretsch in Bozen

Castelforte im Eisacktal

Grundriß

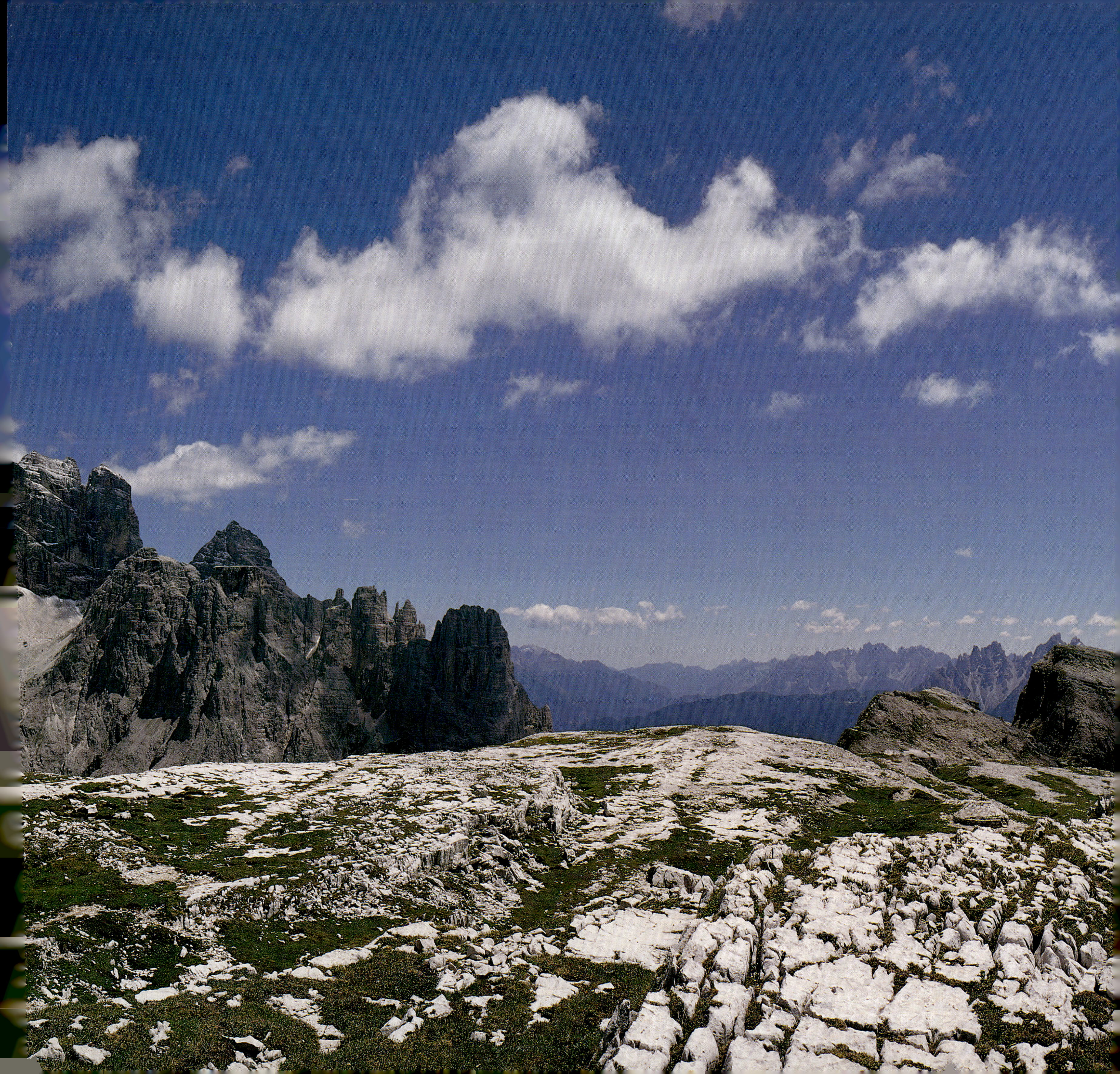

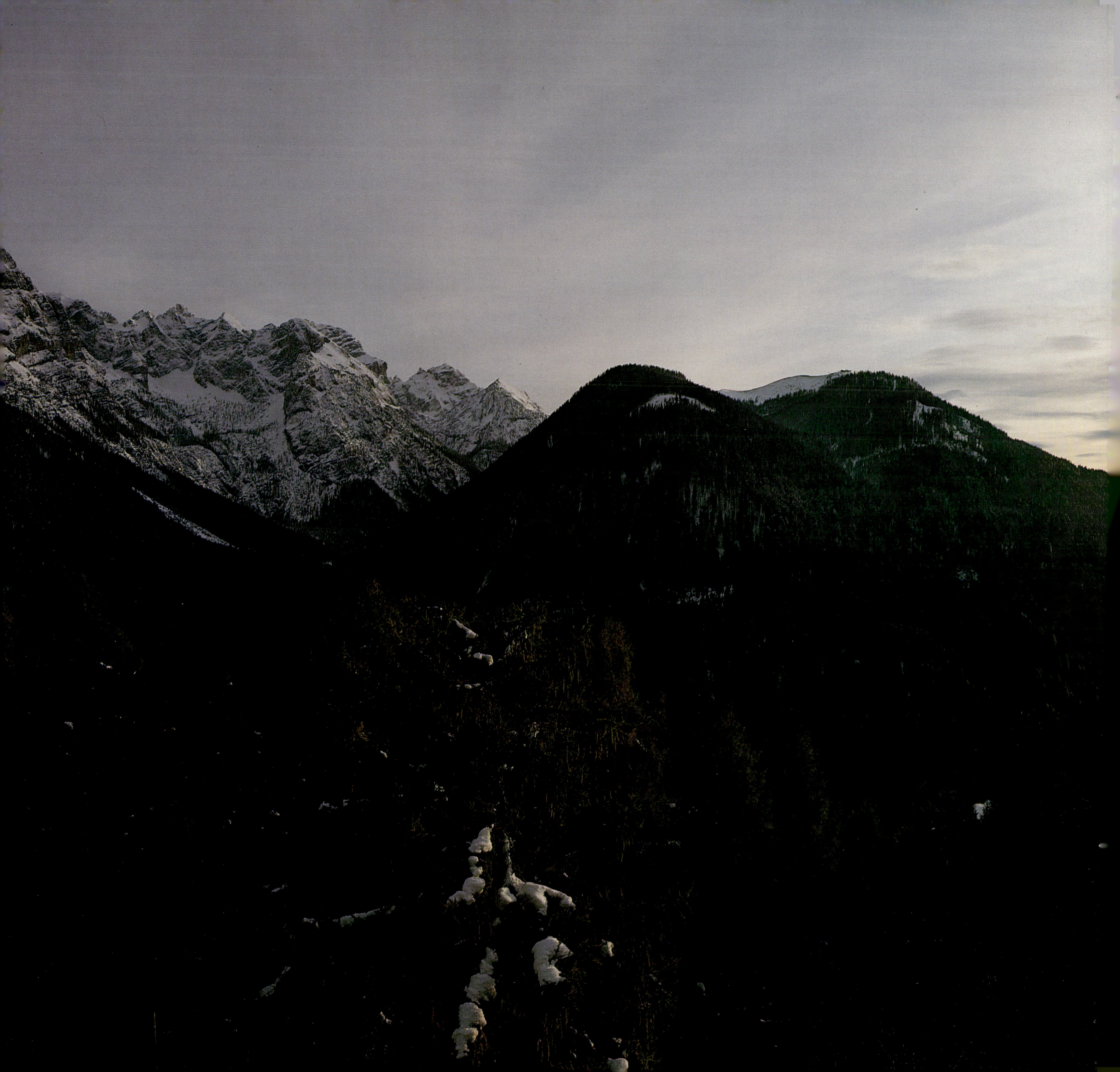

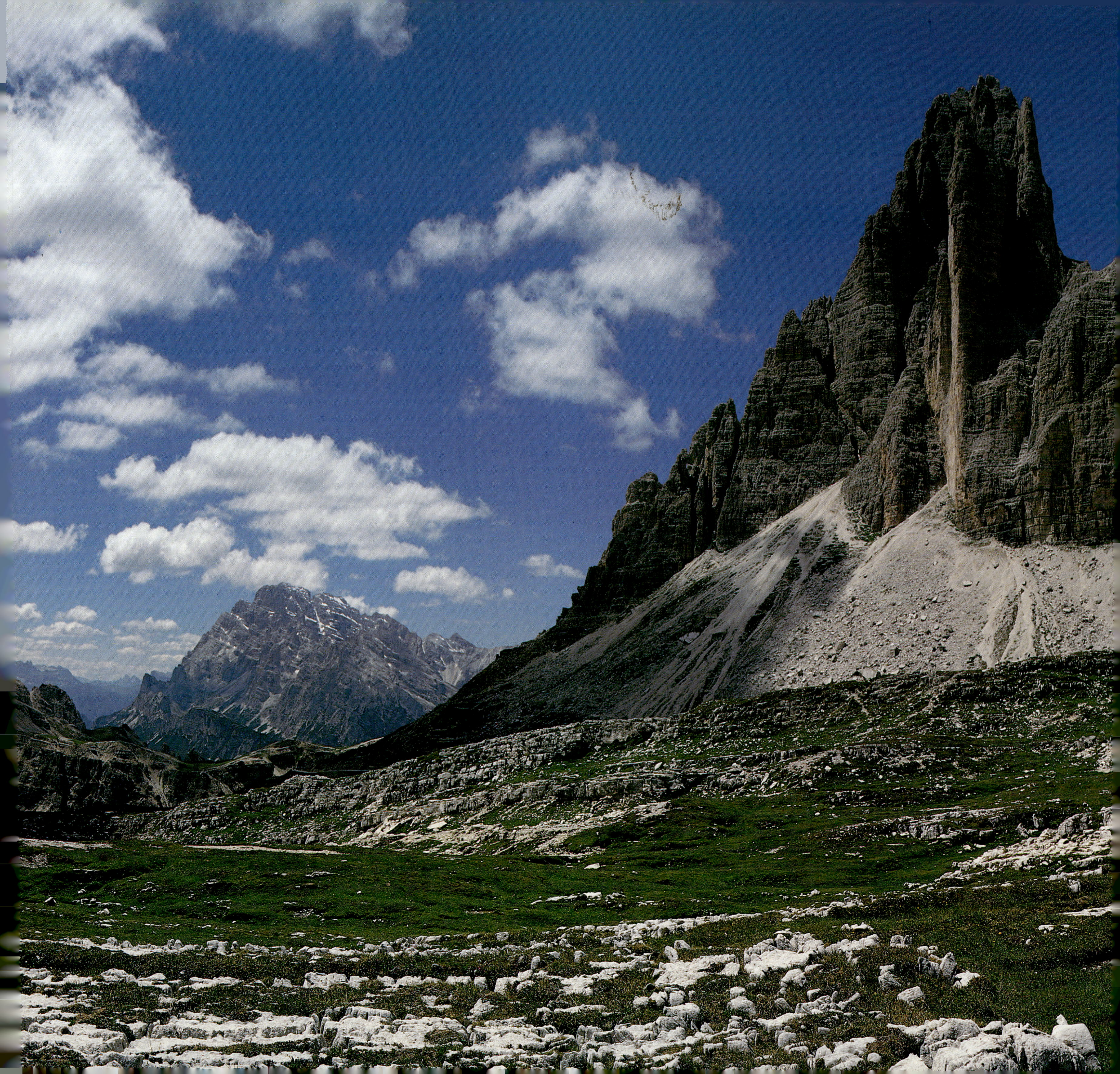

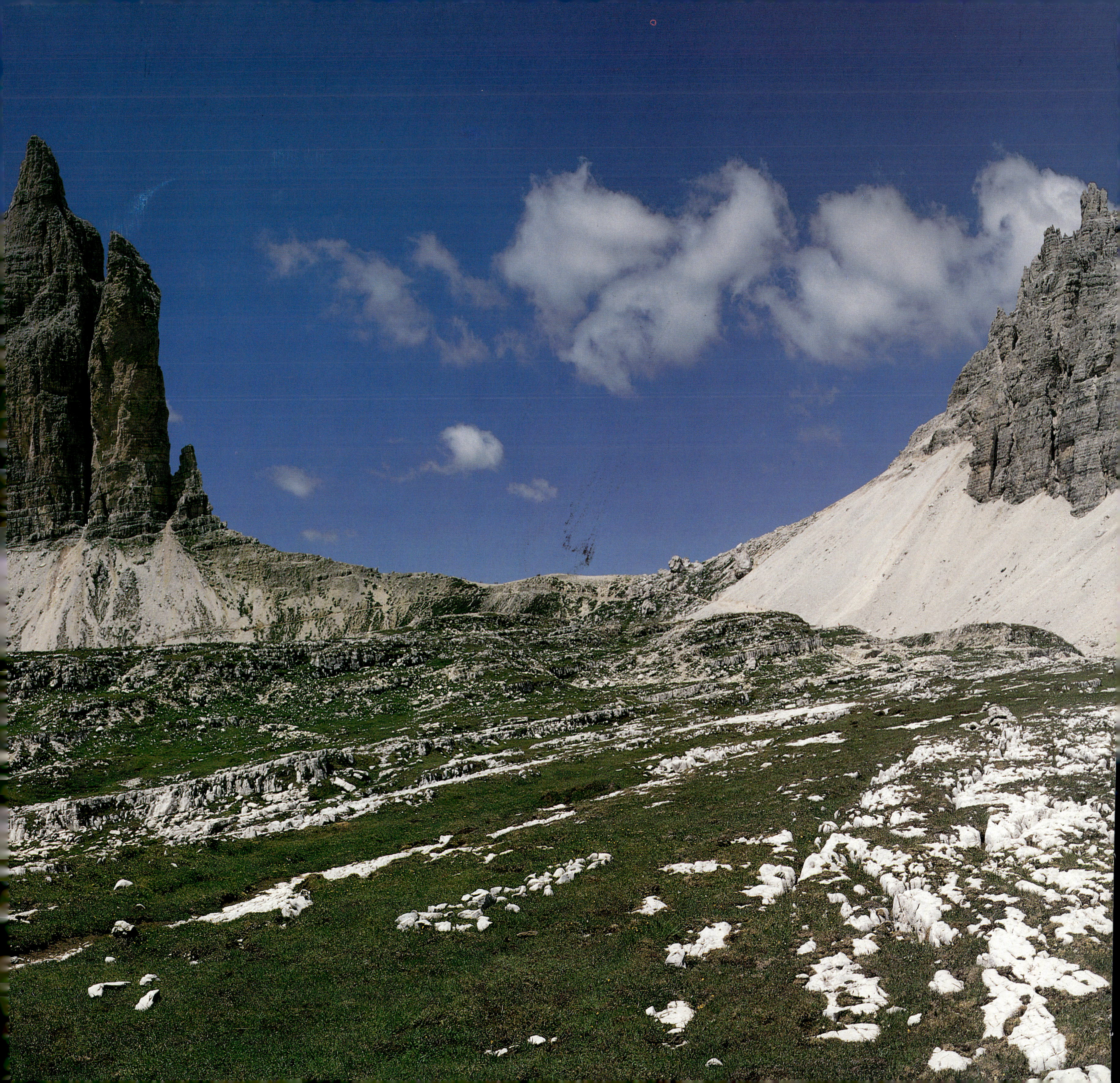

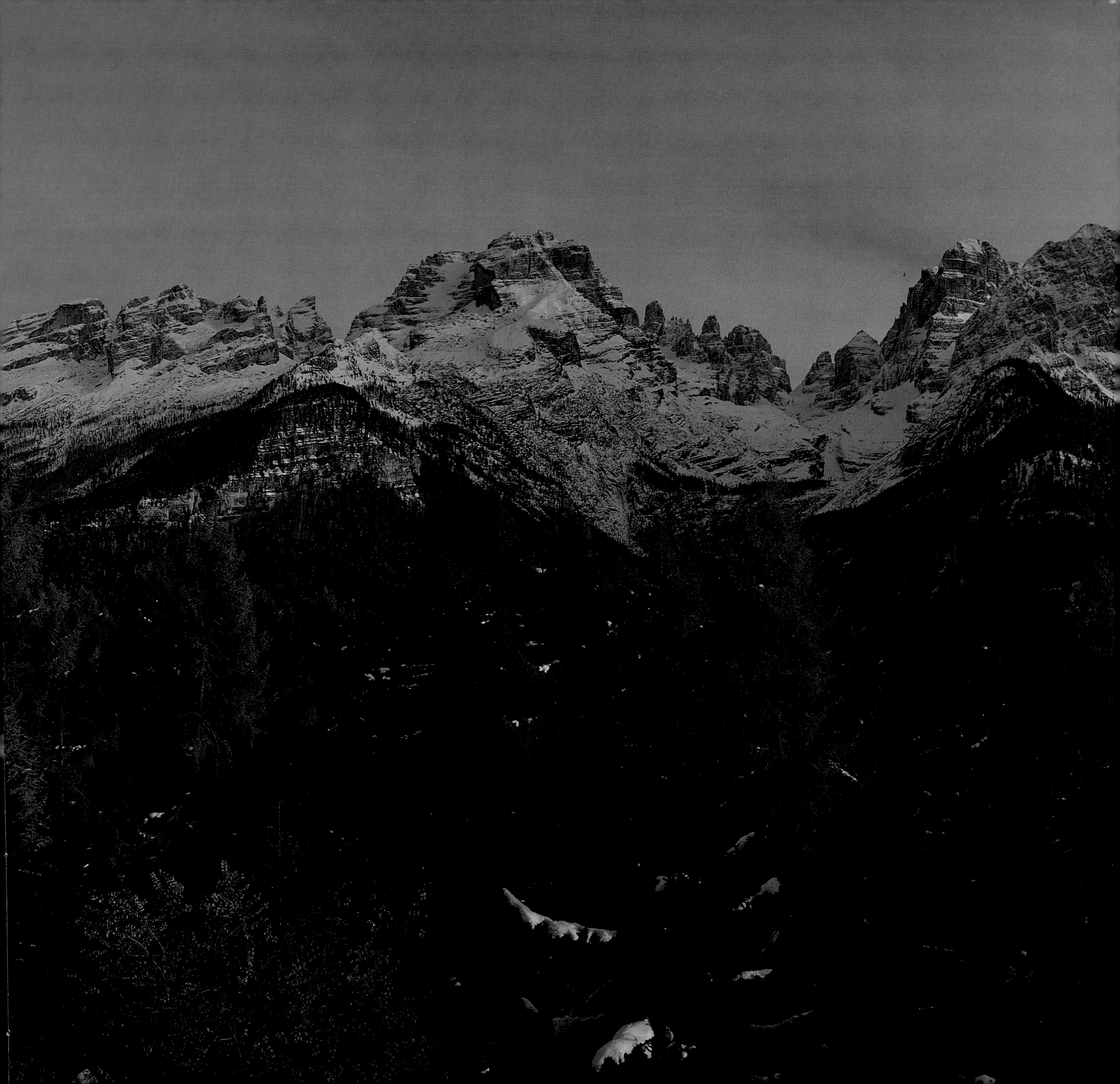

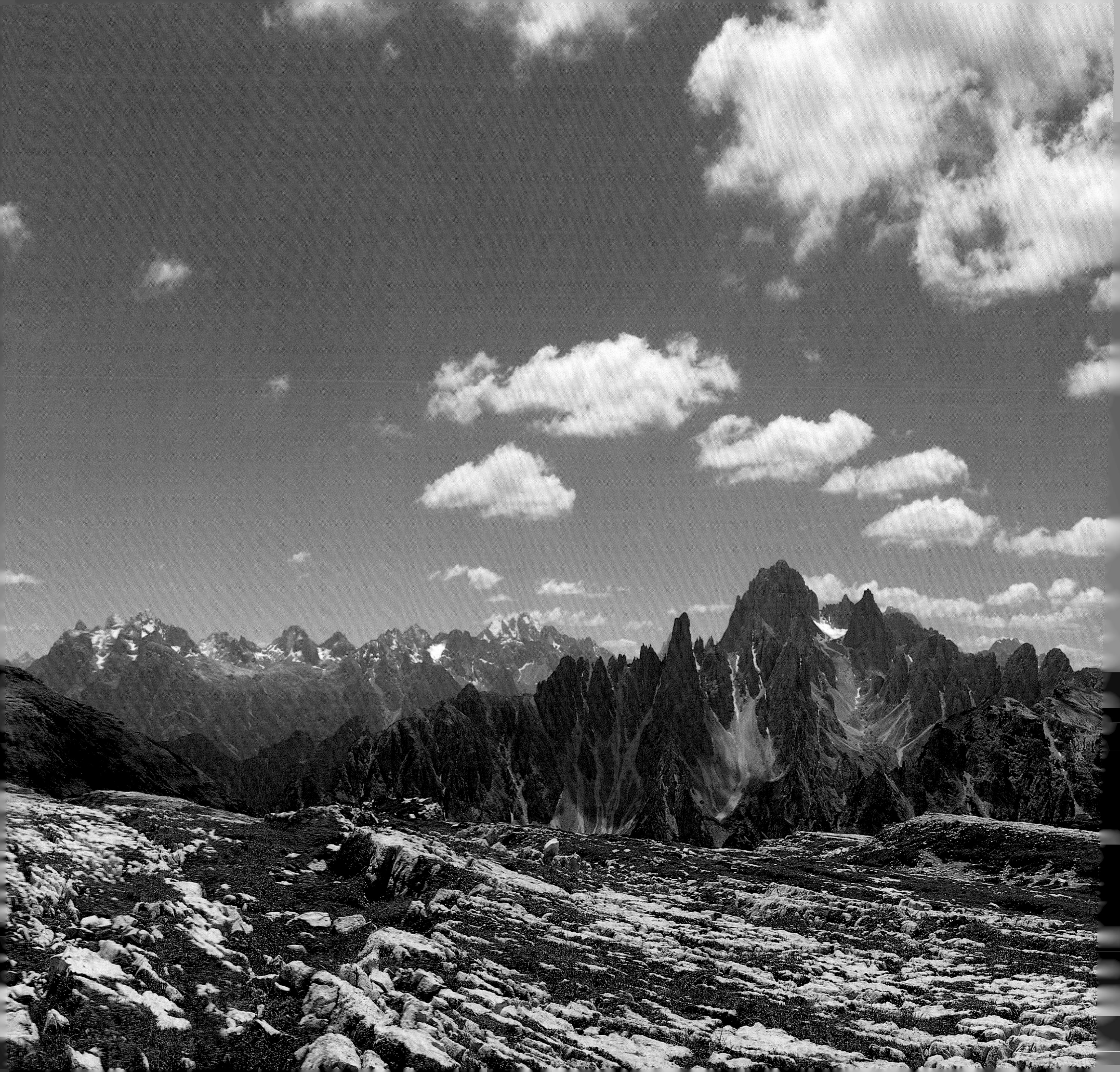

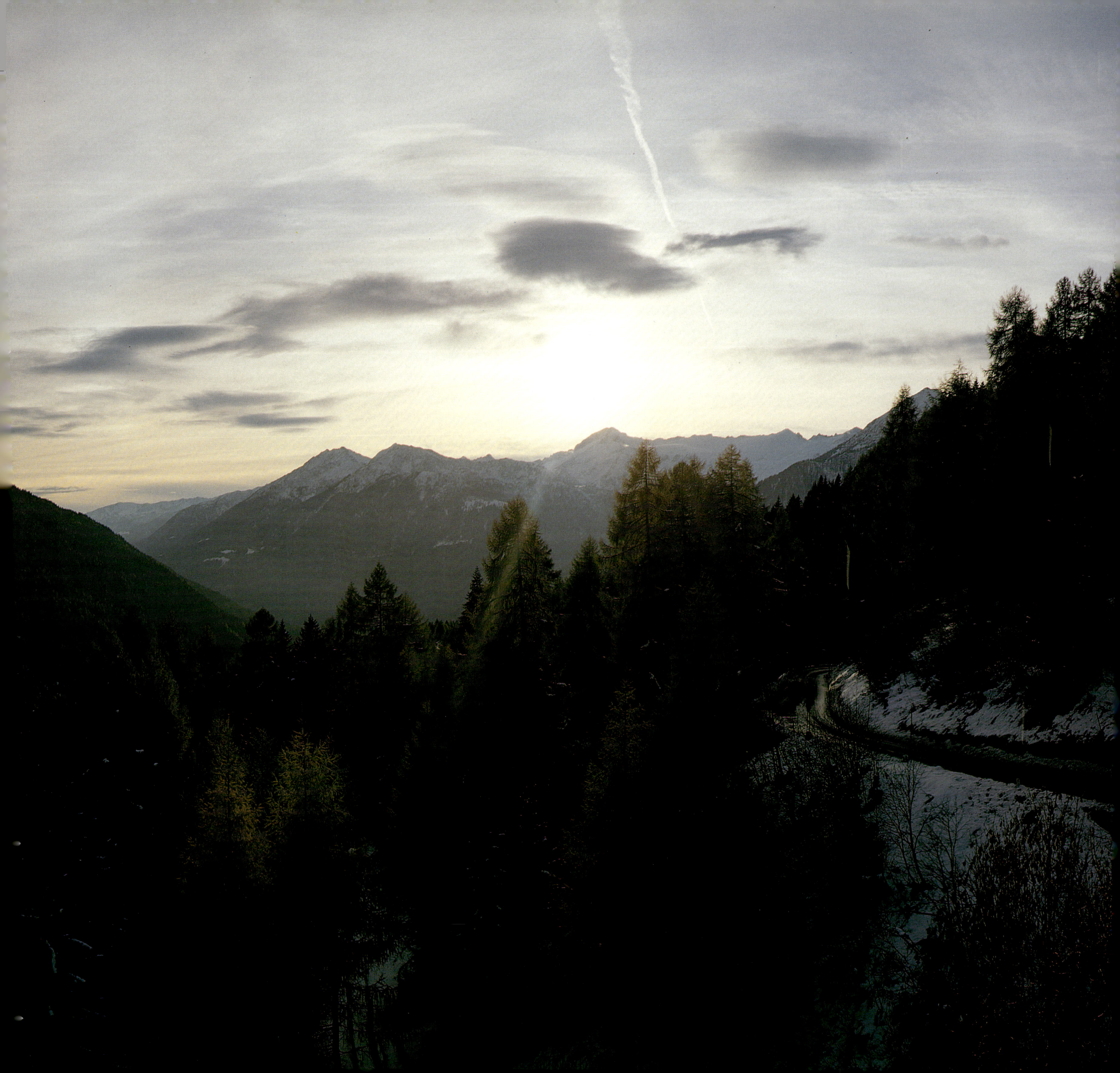

41.
42.

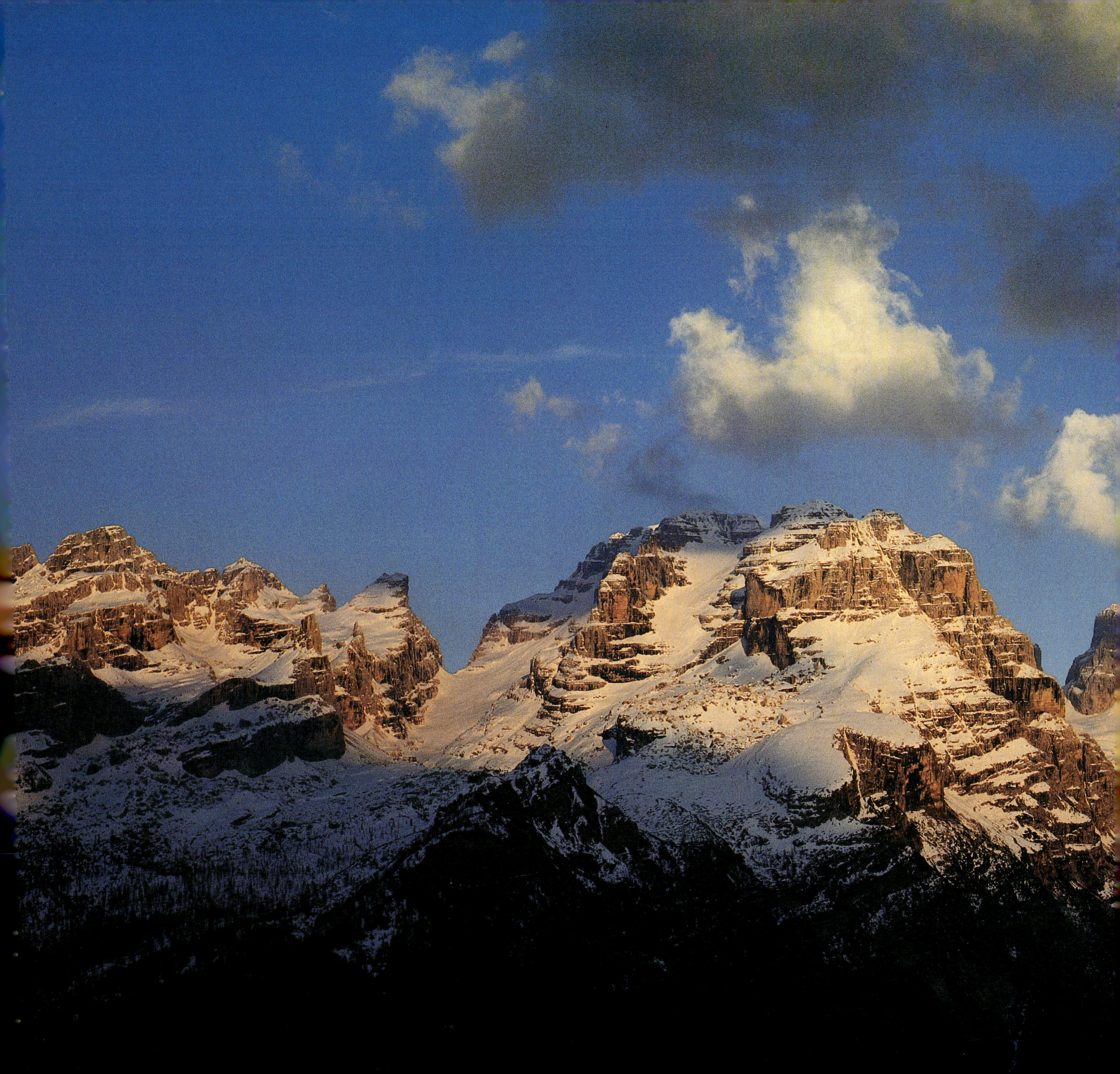

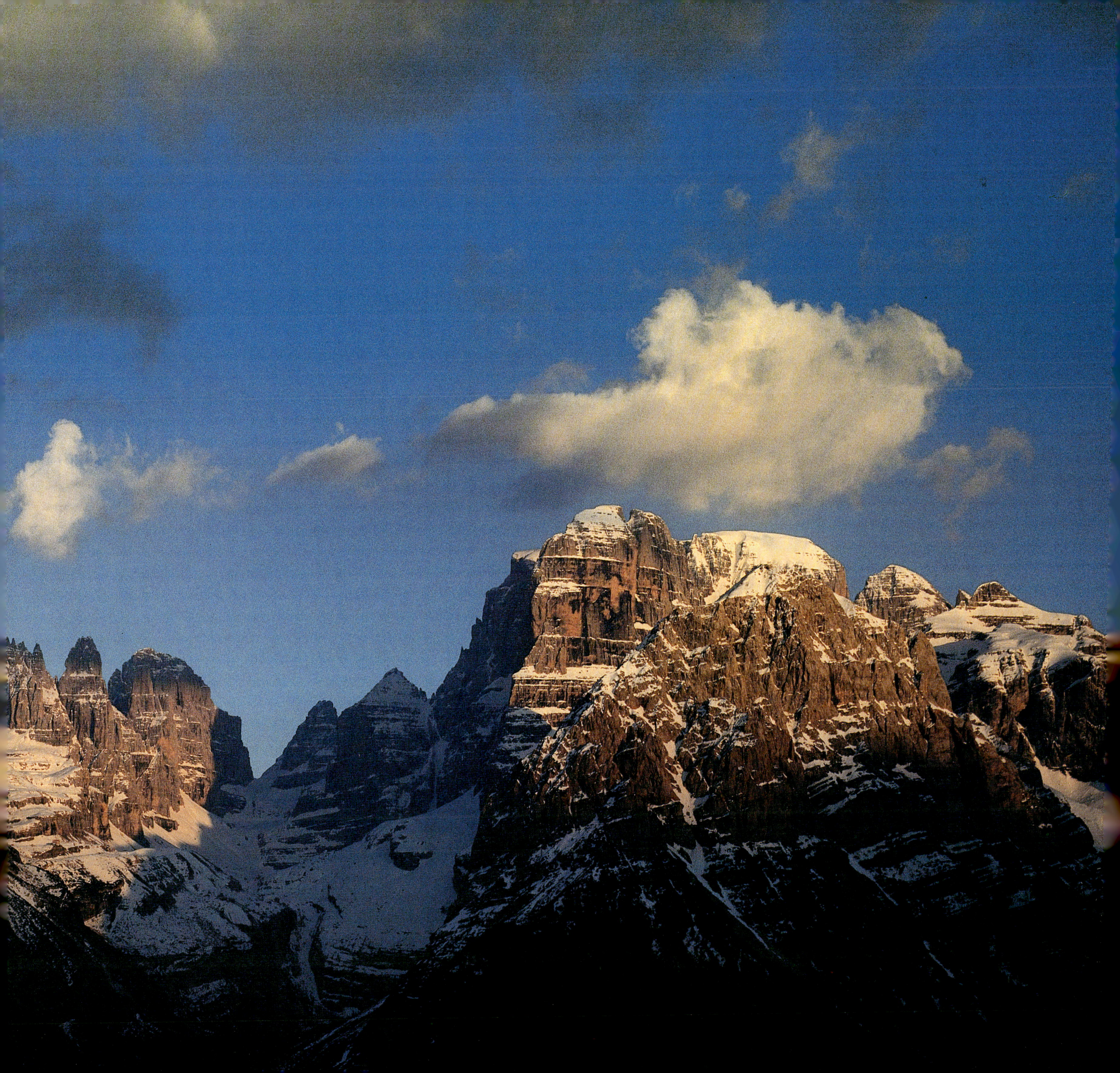

40. Marmarole, Cadinspitzen, Cristallo, Drei Zinnen, Passportenkopf, Elferkofel und Zwölferkofel.
Marmarole, Cadini di Misurina, Cristallo, Cime di Lavaredo, Croda del Passaporto, Cima Undici e Croda dei Toni in una panoramica a 360°.
A 360° panorama of Marmarole, Cadini di Misurina, Cristallo, Cime di Lavaredo, Croda del Passaporto, Cima Undici and Croda dei Toni.
Marmarole, Cadini de Misurina, Cristallo, Sommets de Lavaredo, Croda du Passaporto, Sommet Undici et Croda dei Toni en une vue panoramique à 360°.
Marmarole, Cadini de Misurina, Cristallo, Cimas de Lavaredo, Roca del Pasaporte, Cima Once y Roca de los Toni en una panorámica de 360°.
Мармаролэ, Кадини ди Мизурина, Кристалло, вершины Лаваредо, Крода дель Пассапорто, Сима Ундичи и Крода дей Тони в панорамном виде на 360°.
360°パノラマ写真によるマルマローレ、カディーニ・ディ・ミズリーナ、クリスタッロ、チーマ・ディ・ラヴァレード、クローダ・デル・パッサポールト、チーマ・ウンディチ、クローダ・ディ・トーニの山々

41. Blick auf die Brentagruppe von Madonna di Campiglio.
Madonna di Campiglio. Gruppo di Brenta.
Мадонна ди Кампильо. Группа Брента.
マドンナ・ディ・カンピーリオ。　ブレンタ山群

42. Die Brenta von Molveno aus gesehen.
Gruppo di Brenta. Versante di Molveno.
The Molveno side of the Brenta Group.
Groupe du Brenta. Versant de Molveno.
Grupo del Brenta. El declive de Molveno.
Группо дель Брента. Склон Мольвено.
ブレンタ山群。　モルヴェント側

43. Sonnenuntergang in der Brenta.
Enrosadira sul Gruppo di Brenta.
Alpenglow on the Brenta Group.
Enrosadira sur le Groupe du Brenta.
Enrosadira en el Grupo del Brenta.
Енросадира на группе Брента.
バラ色に染まるブレンタ山群

44. Sass da Ciampac und Sass Songher bei Corvara im Gadertal.
Corvara in Badia. Sass da Ciampac, Sassónghēr.
Корвара ин Бадия. Сасс ди Чиампай и Сассонгер.
バディーアのコルヴァーラ村。　サッス・ディ・チァンパイとサッソンゲール.

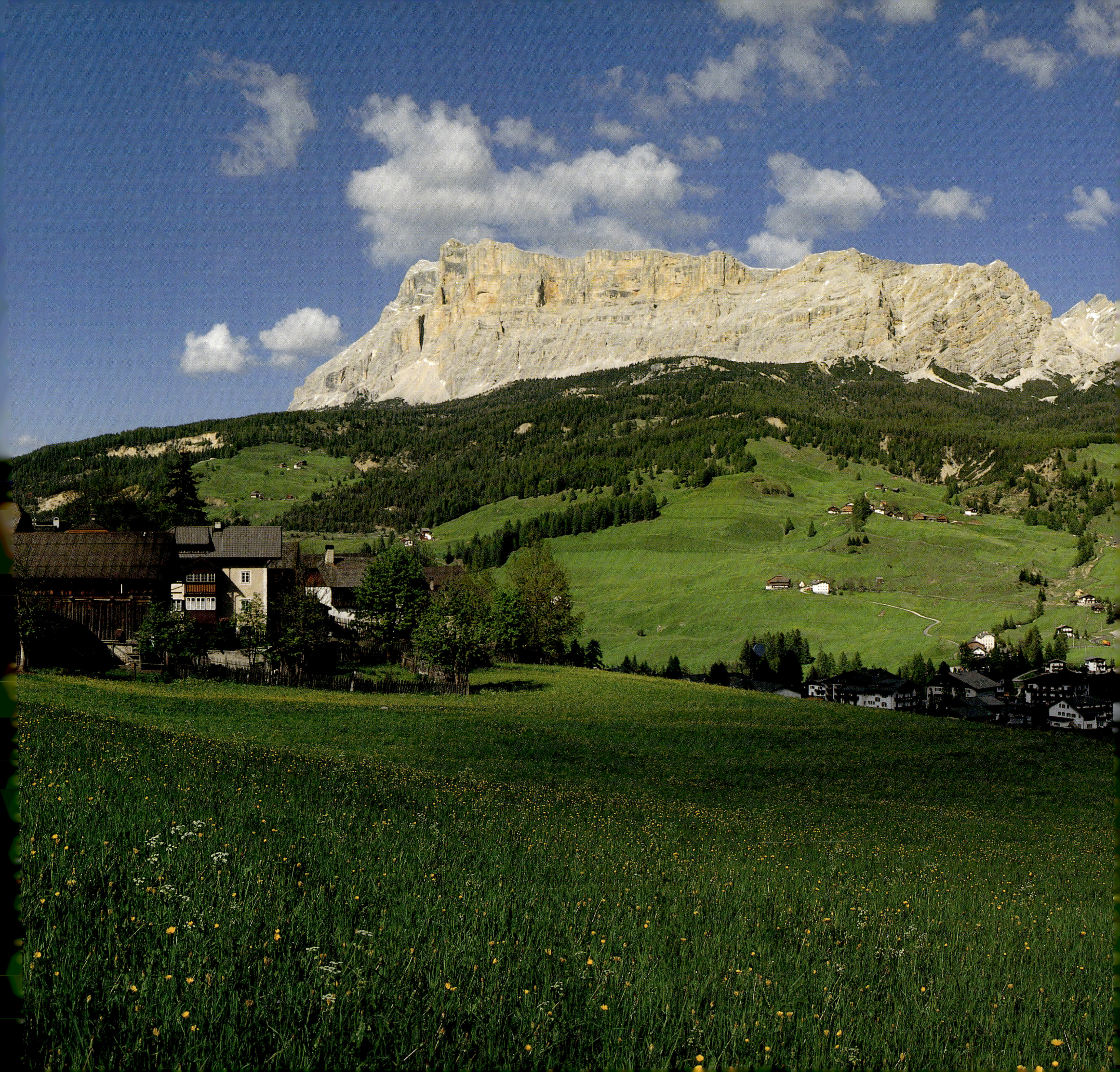

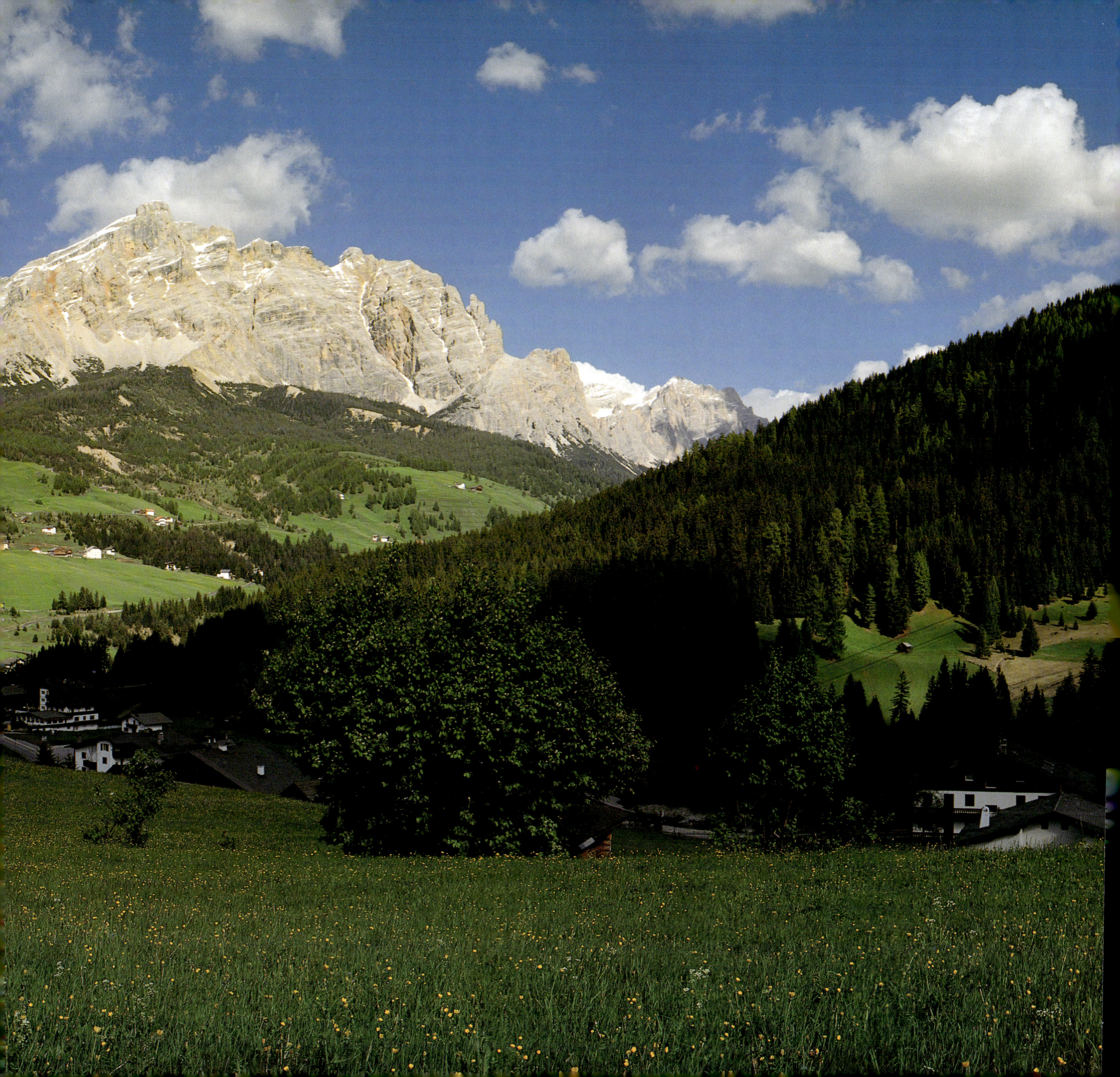

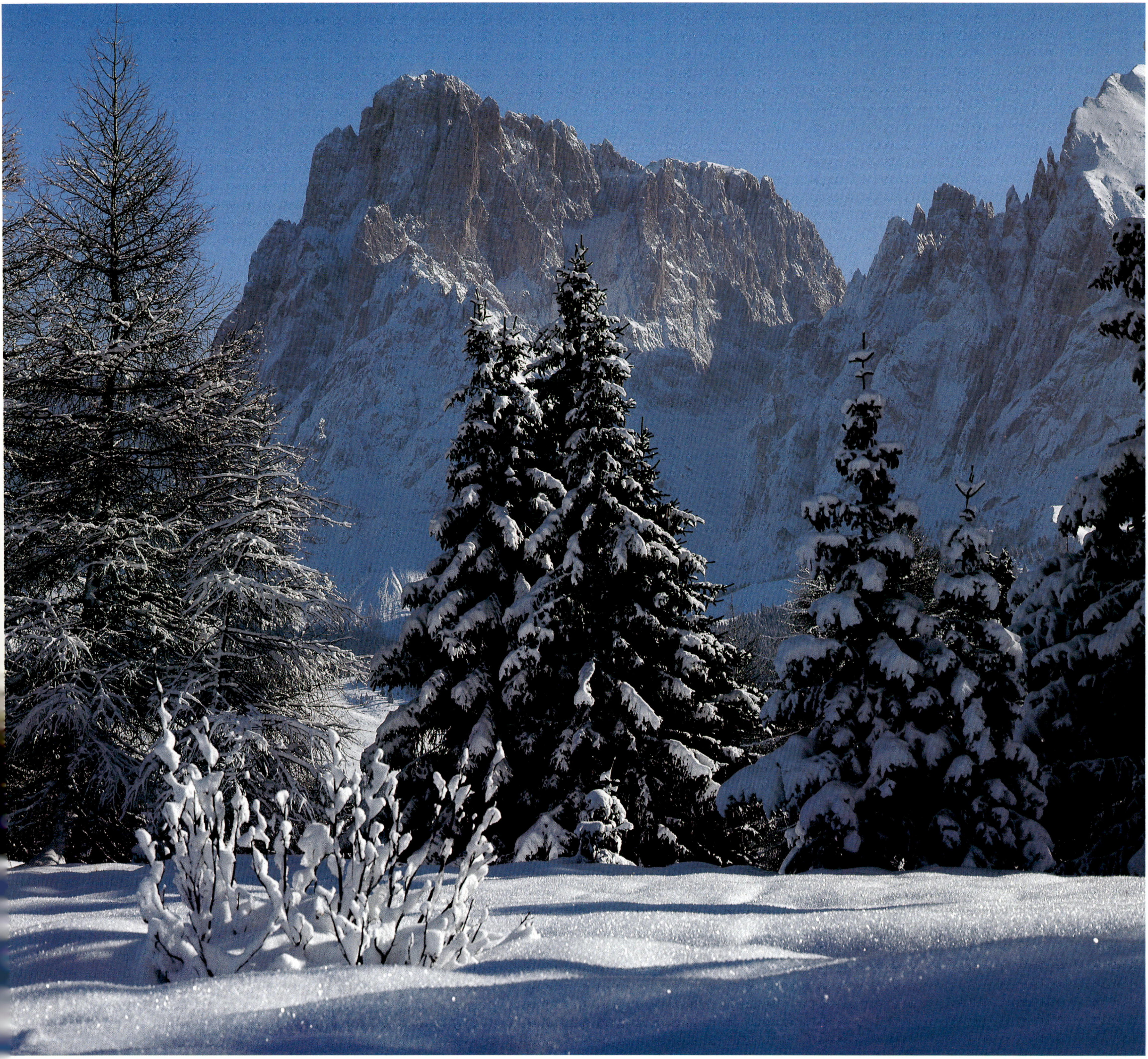

45. Kreuzkofel von Stern im Gadertal aus gesehen.
Val Badia. Sasso della Croce da La Villa.
Val Badia. The Sasso della Croce from the Villa.
Val Badia. Sasso de la Croce de La Villa.
Valle Badia. Peña de la Cruz de La Villa.
Долина Бадия. Сассо делла Кроче де ла Вилла.
バディーア谷。　クローチェ・ダ・ラ・ヴィッラ

46. Seiser Alm. Langkofel.
Alpe di Siusi. Sassolungo.
Альпы Сьюзи. Сассолунго.
スィウーズィの放牧小屋

47. Völs am Schlern.
Fié allo Sciliar.
Фиè алло Счилиар.
フィエー・アッロ・スィッリアール

48. Am Schlern.
Altopiano di Sciliar.
Горный рельеф Счилиар.
スィッリアールの高地

49. Seiser Alm.
Alpe di Siusi.
Альпы Сьюзи.
スィウーズィの放牧小屋

50. Alphornbläser in Marinzen bei Kastelruth.
Marinzen di Castelrotto. Corni alpini.
Marinzen di Castelrotto. Alpenhorns.
Marinzen de Castelrotto. Cors alpins.
Marinzen de Castelrotto. Cuernos alpinos.
Маринцен ди Кастелротто. Альпийские Роги.
マリンゼン・ディ・カステルロット。　角笛

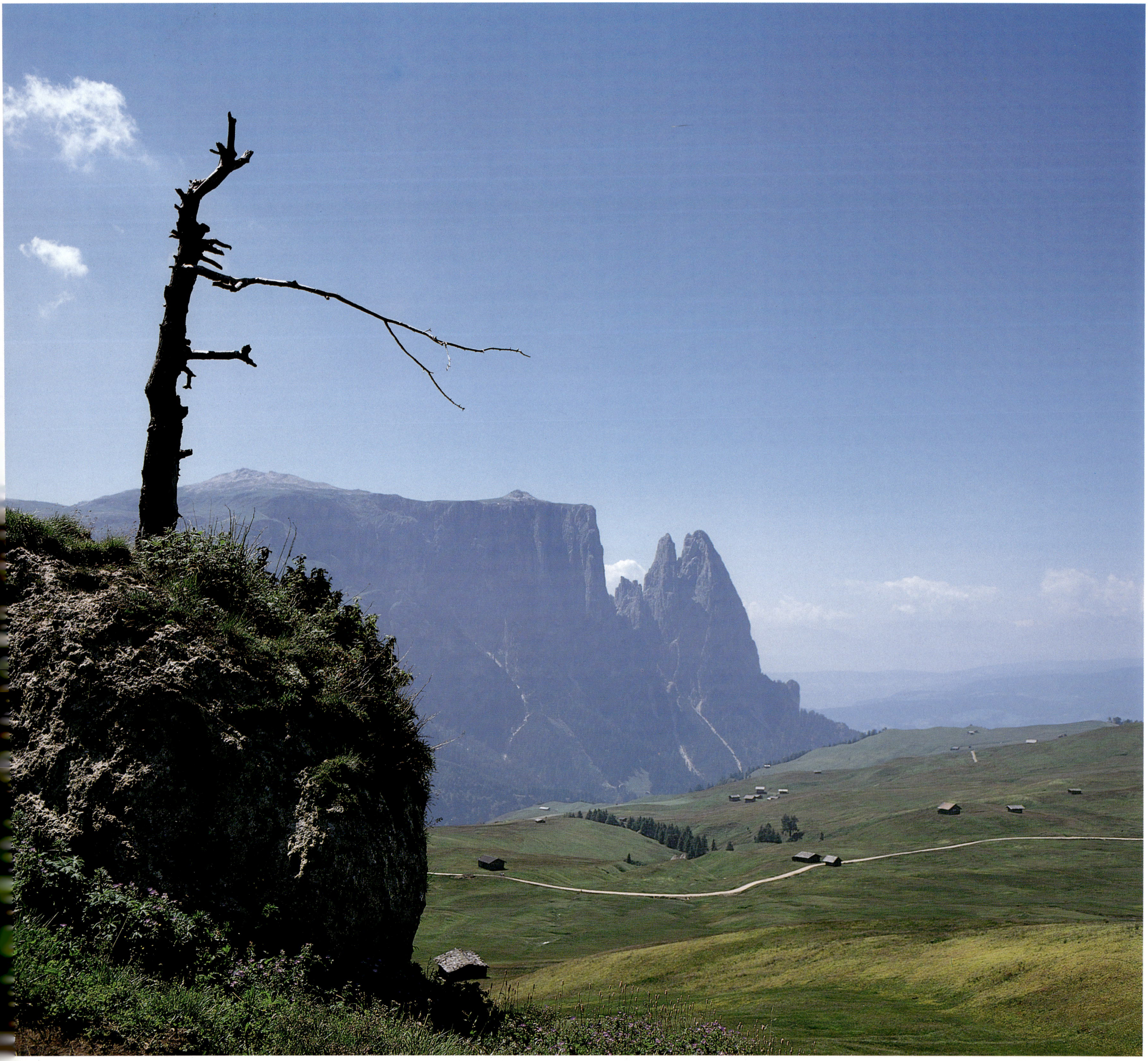

50.

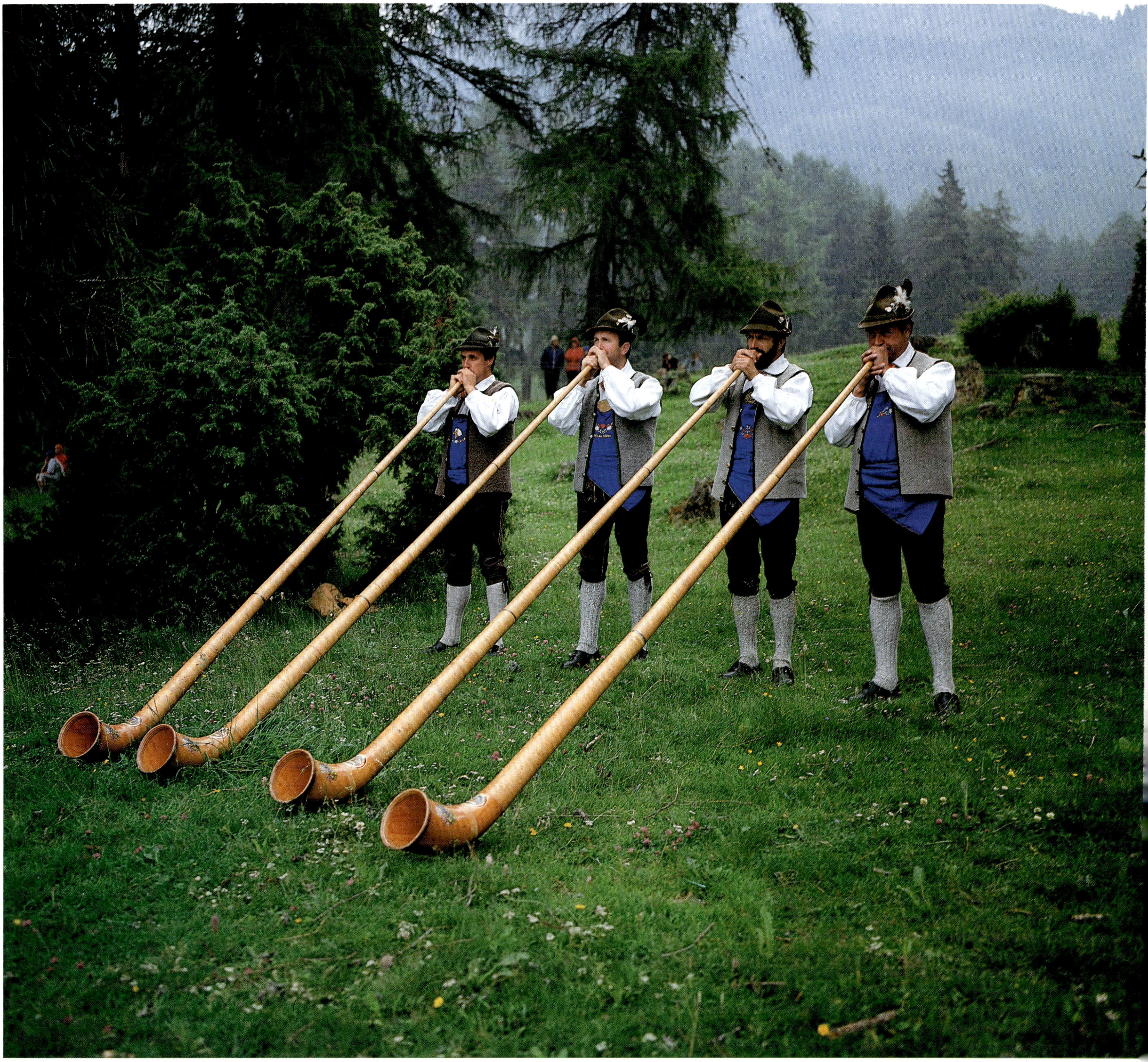

1.

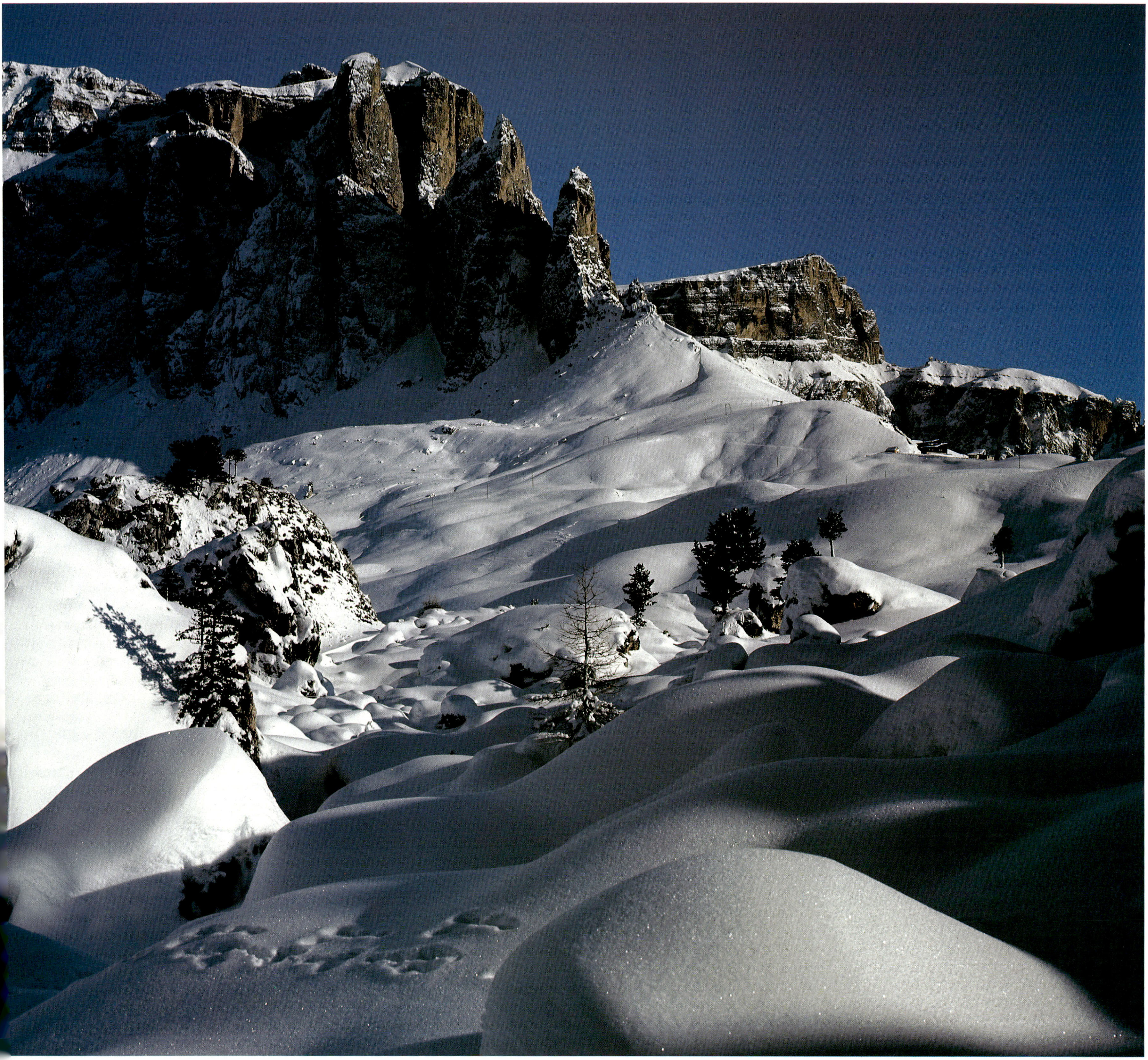

51. Sellatürme und Pordoispitze vom Sellajoch aus gesehen.
Passo Sella. Torri di Sella, Sass Pordoi.
Перевал Сэлла. Башни Сэлла. Сасс Пордой.
セッラ峠。　トーリ・ディ・セッラとサッス・ポルドーイ

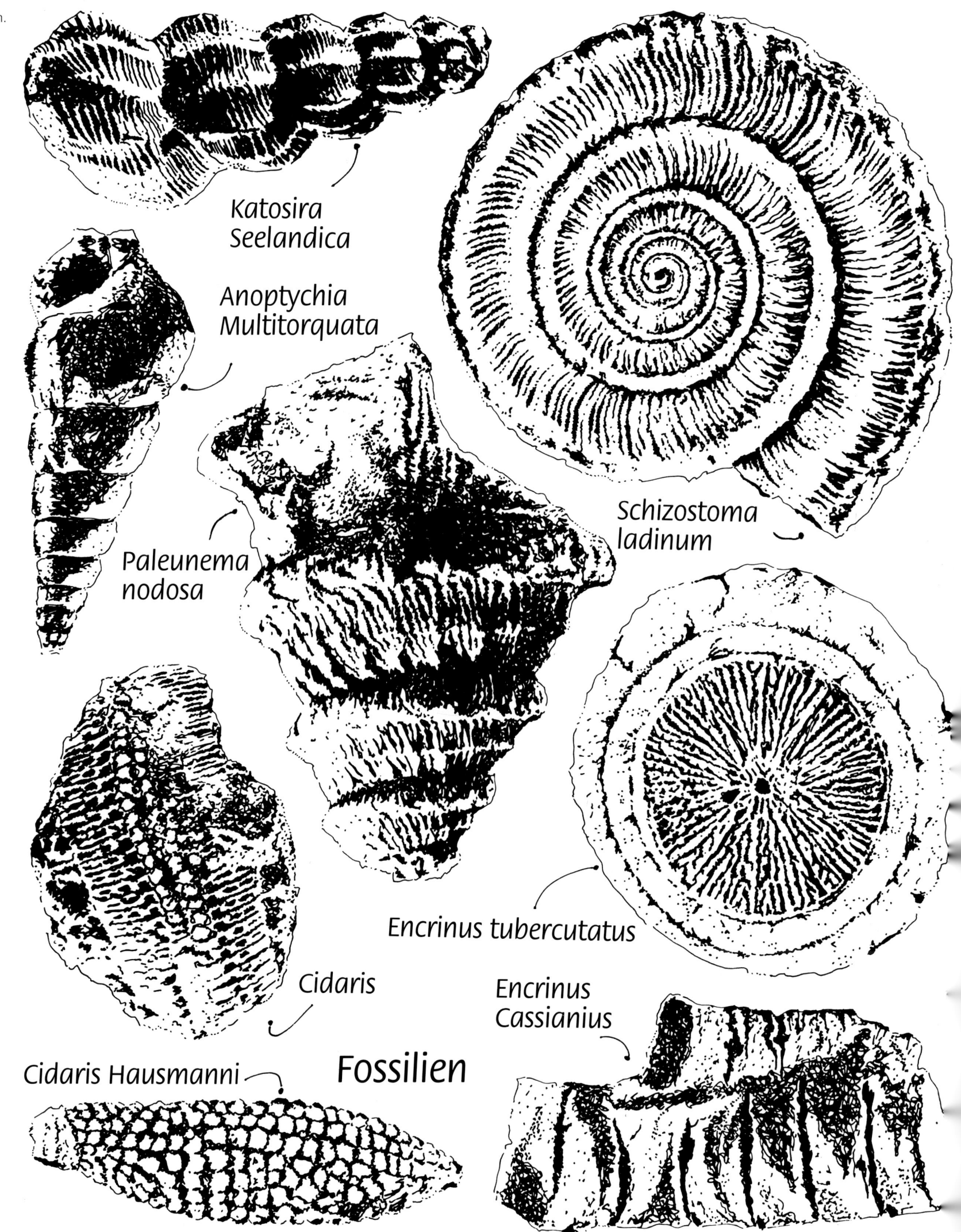

Katosira Seelandica

Anoptychia Multitorquata

Schizostoma ladinum

Paleunema nodosa

Encrinus tubercutatus

Cidaris

Encrinus Cassianius

Cidaris Hausmanni

Fossilien

52. Langkofelgruppe, Geislerspitzen, Sellatürme, Pordoispitze und Marmolata vom Sellajoch gesehen.
Passo Sella. Sassolungo, Odle, Torri di Sella, Sass Pordoi, Marmolada.
Перевал Сэлла. Сассолунго, Одлэ, Башни Сэлла, Сасс Пордой и Мармолада.
セッラ峠。　サッソ・ルンゴ、オードゥレ、トーリ・ディ・セッラ、サッス・ポルドォーイ、マルモラーダ

53. Marmolata.
Marmolada.
Мармолада.
マルモラーダ

54. Canazei im Fassatal.
Val di Fassa. Canazei.
Долина Фасса. Канацей.
ファッサ谷。　カナゼイ

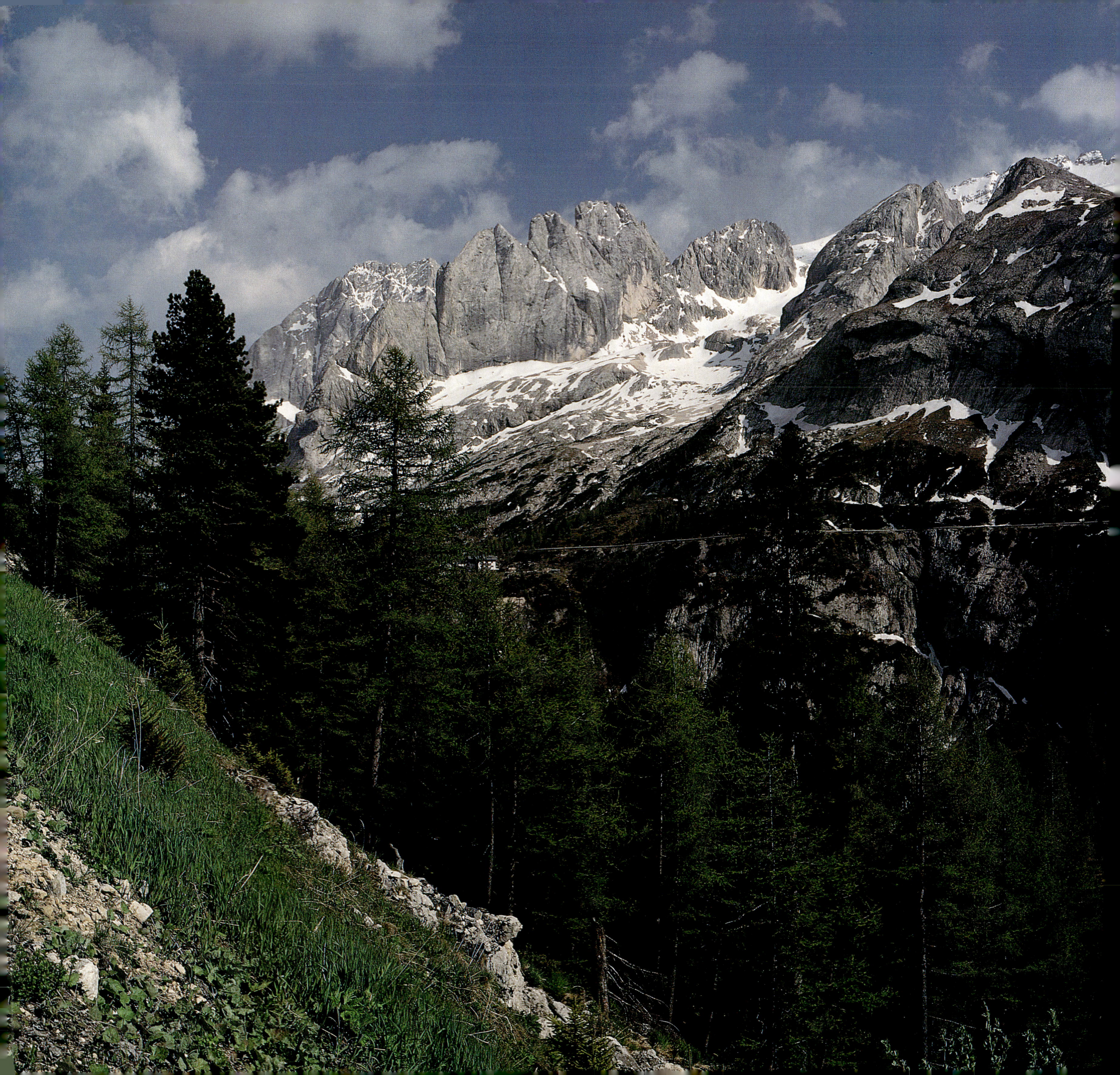

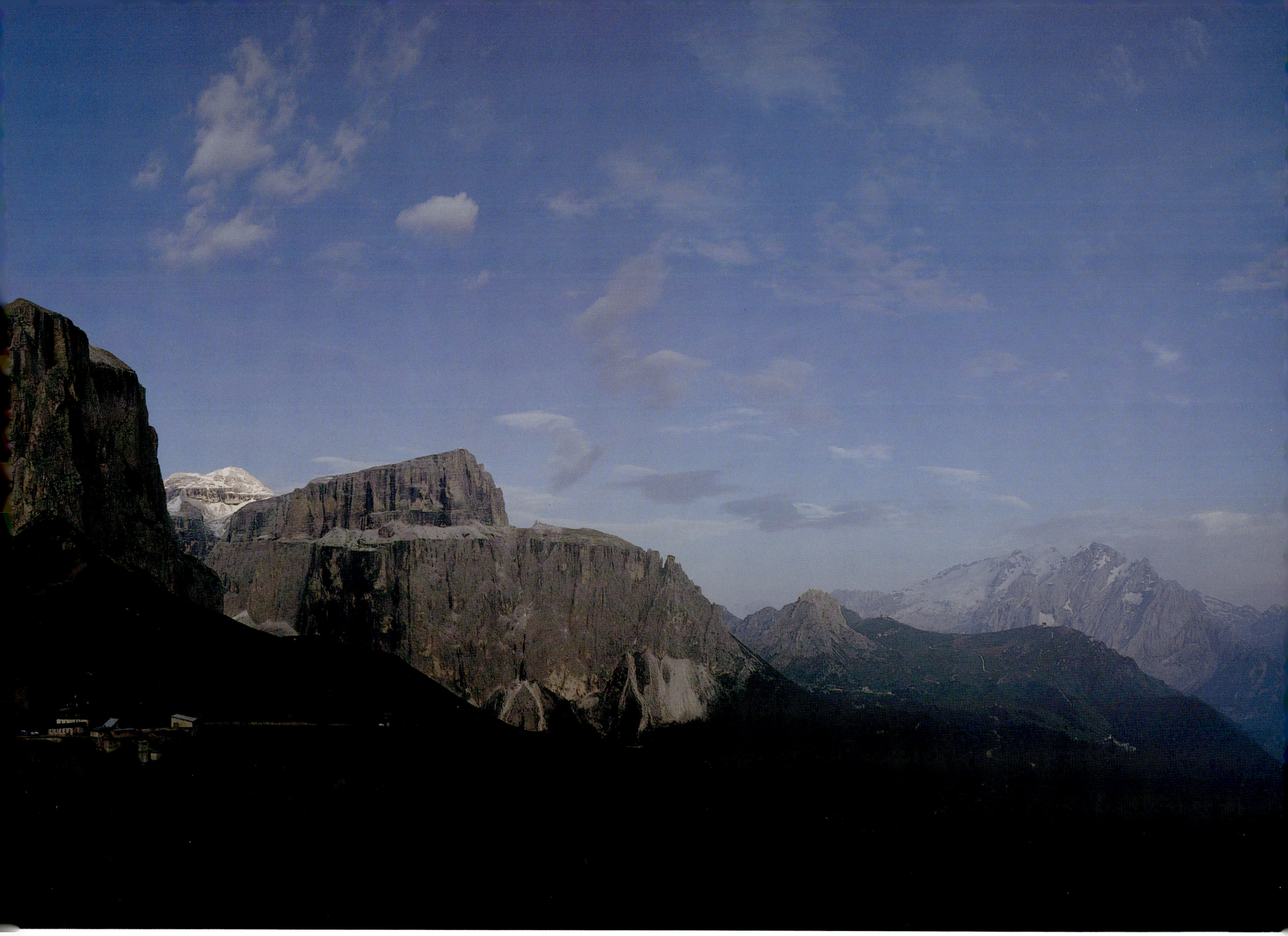

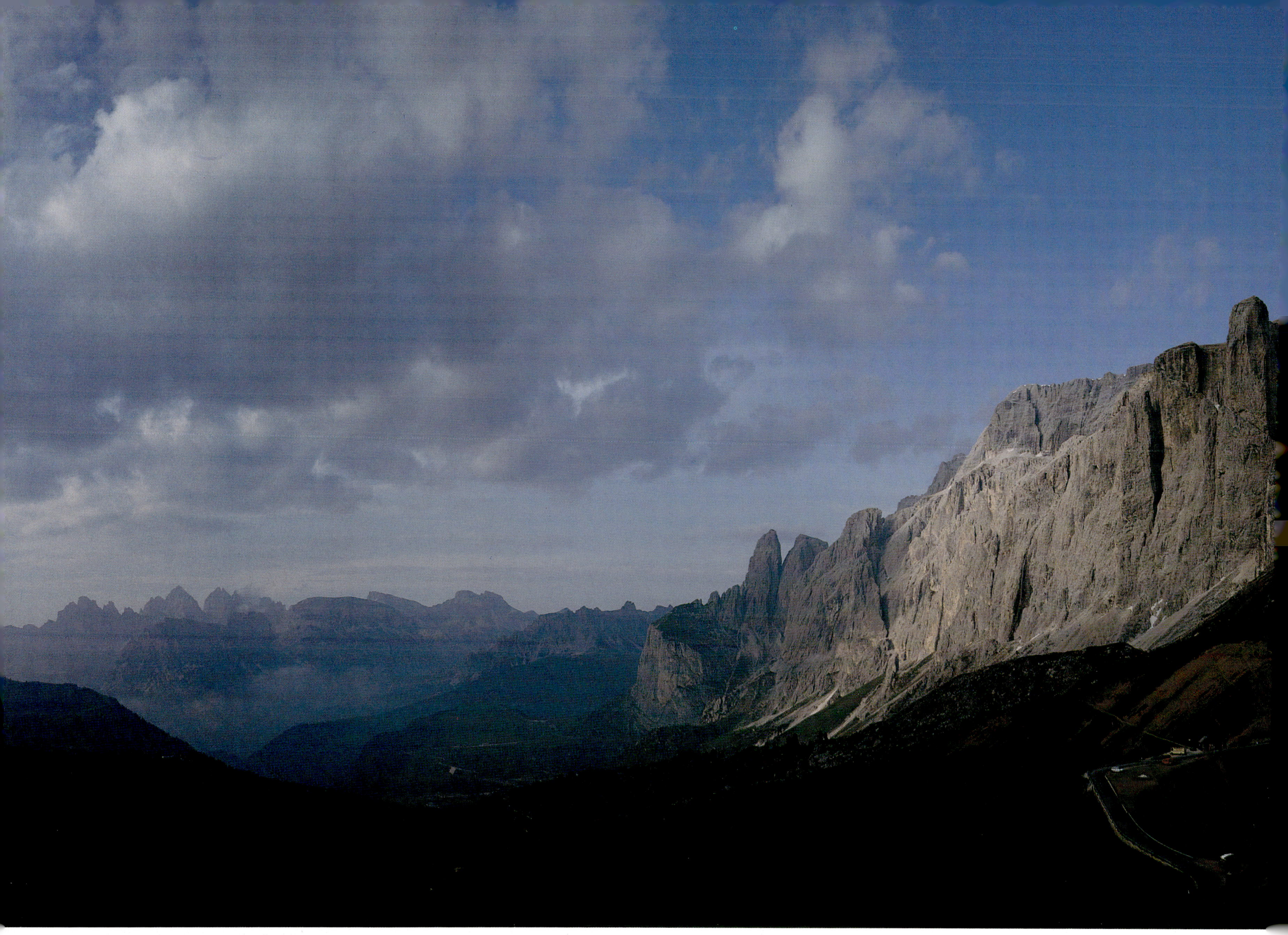

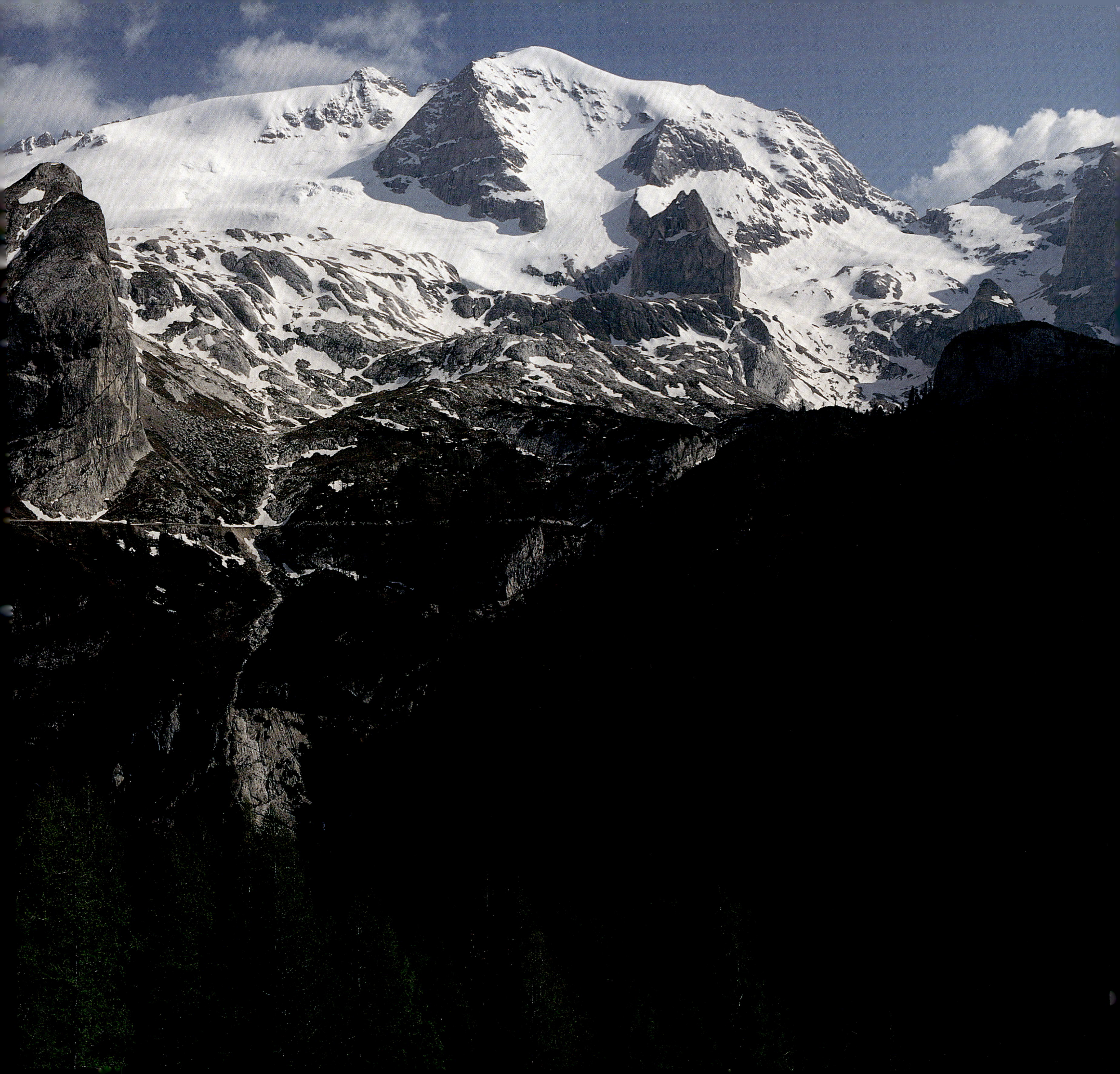

54.

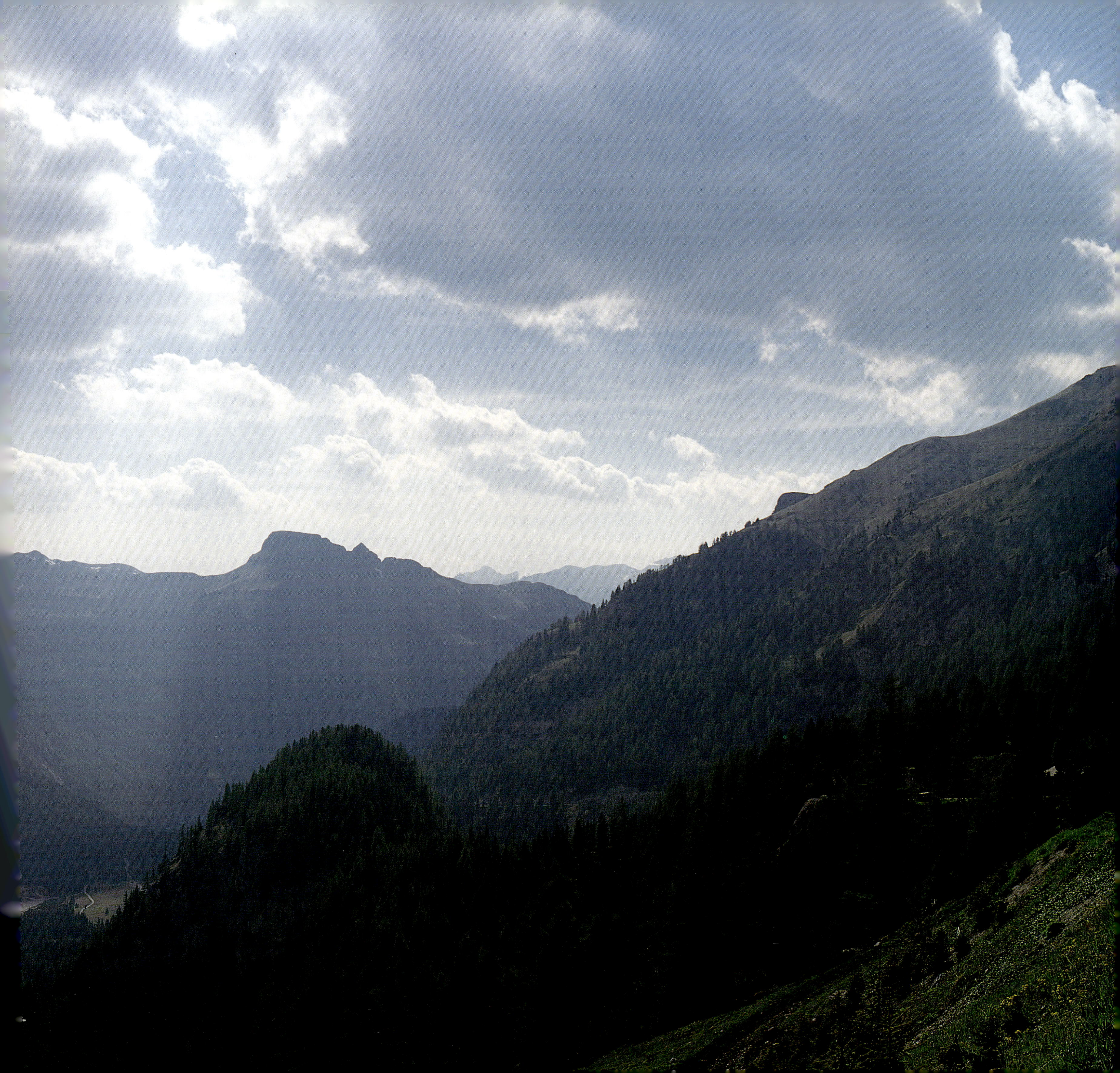

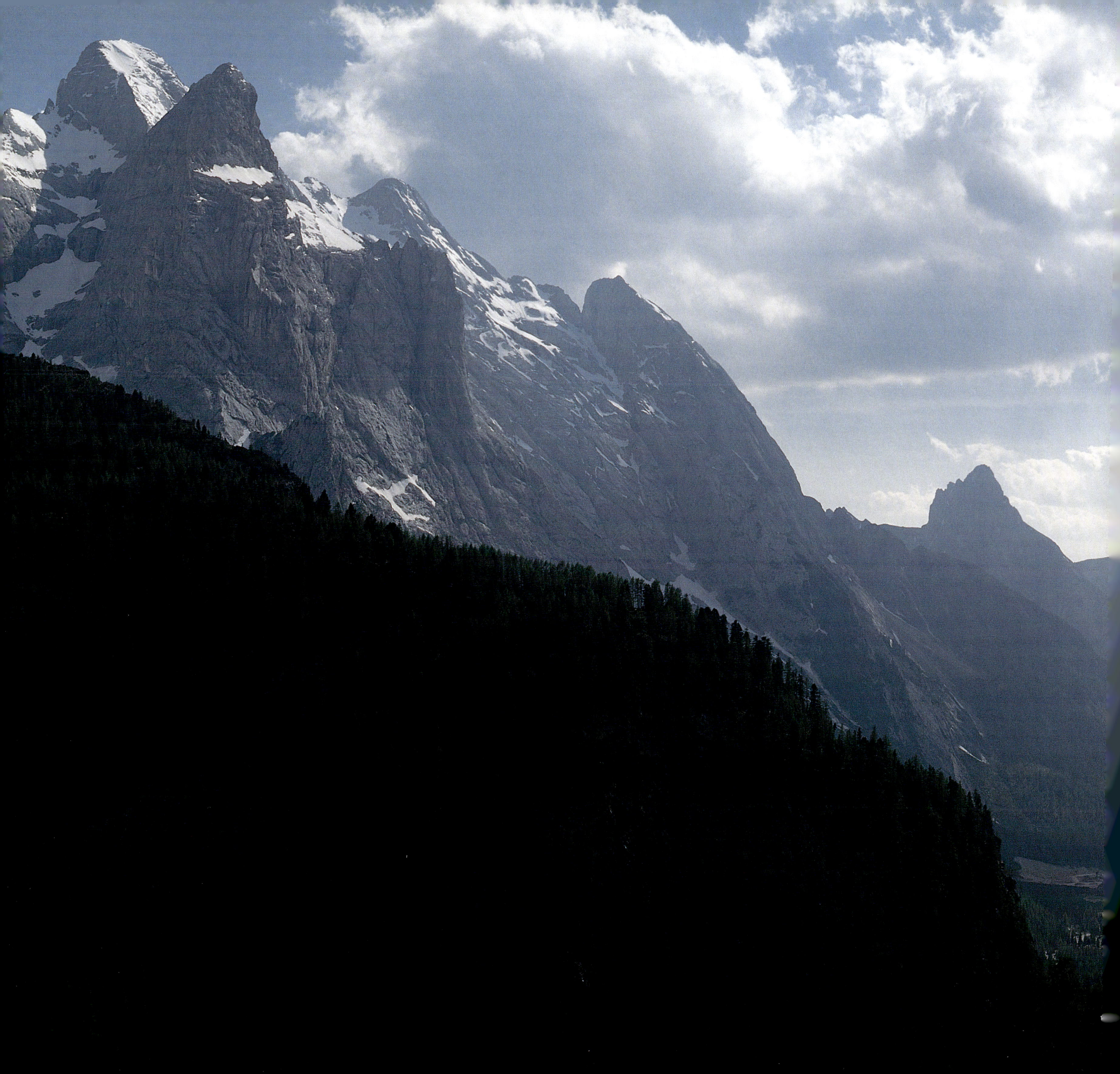

55. Die «Wand der Wände» in der Civetta.
Civetta. La parete delle pareti.
The «wall of walls» on the Civetta.
Civetta. La paroi des parois.
Civetta. La pared de las paredes.
Чиветта. Самая большая стена.
チヴェッタ。　第一級のおりがみ付の壁面

56. Blick von Alleghe auf die Civetta.
Alleghe. Gruppo del Civetta.
Аллеге. Группа Чиветта.
アッレーゲ。　チヴェッタ山群

57. Civetta.
Gruppo del Civetta.
Группа Чиветта.
チヴェッタ山群

58. Pomagagnon bei Cortina d'Ampezzo.
Cortina d'Ampezzo. Pomagagnòn.
Кортина д'Ампеццо. Помаганьон.
コルティーナ・ダンペッツオ。
ポマガニョン

56.

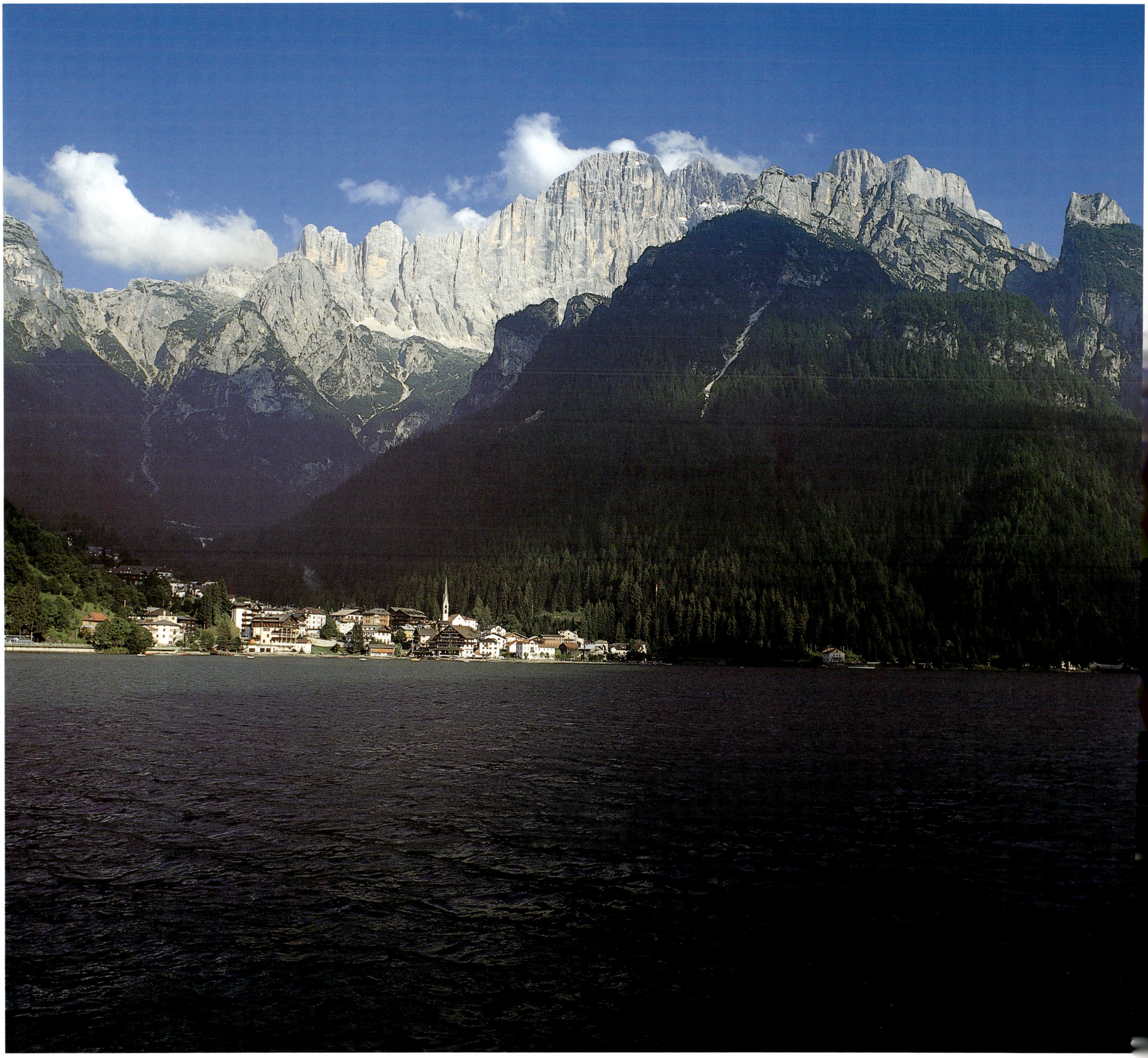

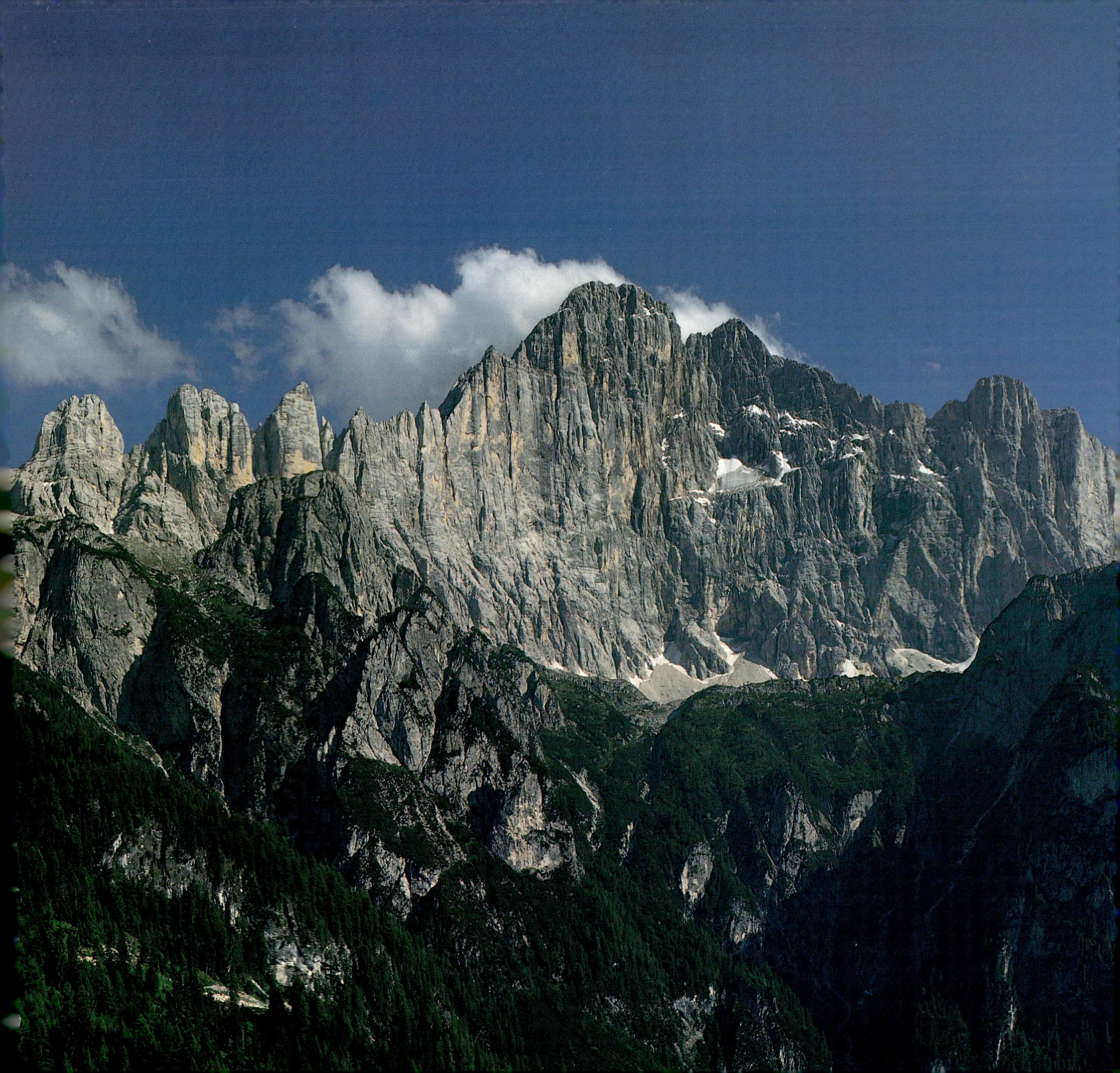

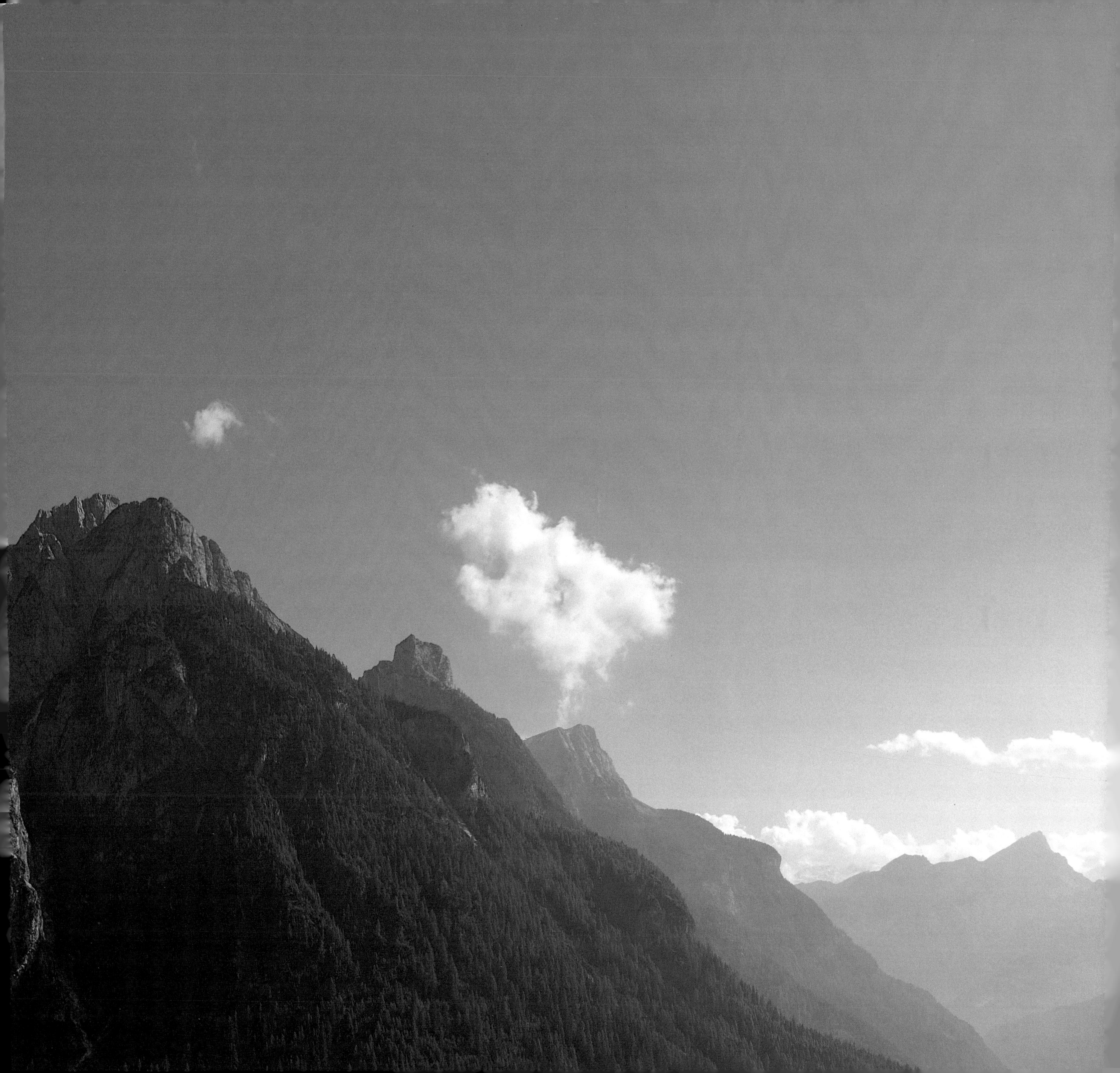

58.

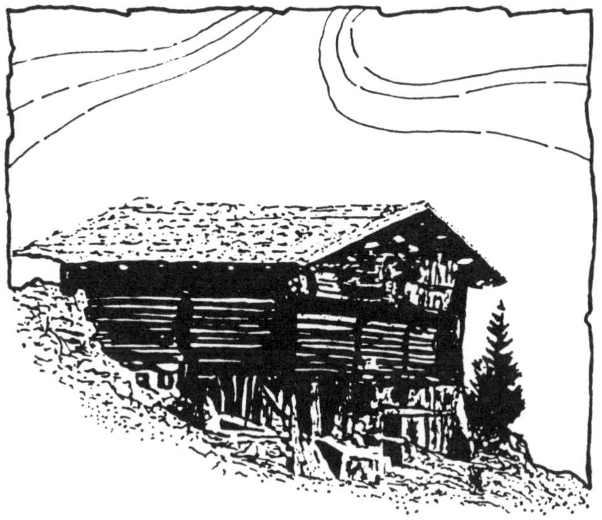
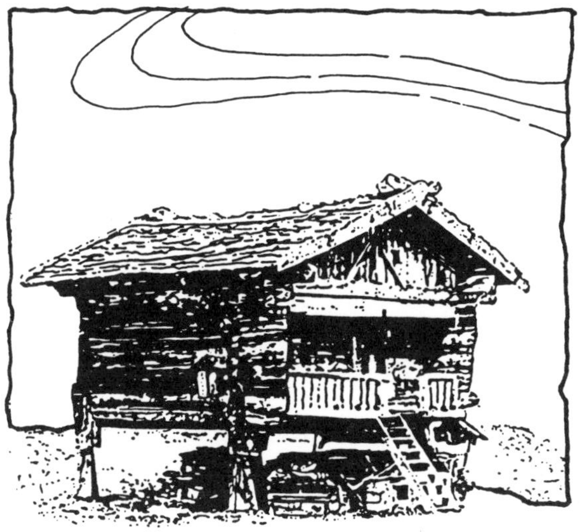

Bildlegenden
Captions

1.

Die Dolomiten sind eine faszinierende Berglandschaft, die in den Alpen einzigartig ist. Obwohl sie, im Vergleich zu anderen Gruppen der Alpen, relativ spät entdeckt wurden, galten sie bald als Dorado für Reisende und Bergsteiger, die auf der Suche nach aufregenden Wegen, nach neuen Horizonten und nach gewagten und scheinbar undurchführbaren Gipfelbesteigungen waren. Nach der naturwissenschaftlichen Entdeckung von Déodat de Dolomieu, der 1788 als erster ihre besondere geologische Zusammensetzung bestimmen konnte, übernahmen die Dolomiten in kürzester Zeit eine Hauptrolle in der Geschichte der Bergwelt. Auf unserer Rundreise lassen wir uns vom Geist der Reisenden von damals führen, als Traum und Wirklichkeit in einer Aura von Zauber und Geheimnis miteinander wetteiferten. Vom Weideland um den Karerpaß führt uns die gelbrote Westwand der Rotwand, im südlichen Teil der Rosengartengruppe gelegen, symbolisch in die Welt voller Felsen und Licht, in die der »Bleichen Berge«, ein.

The Dolomites offer one of the most fascinating and singular landscapes to be found in the Alps. Their »discovery« came rather late in the day compared with that of the other chains. They made up for lost time, however, by staking an immediate claim to a place in the legends of mountaineering as the Mecca for both climbers and travellers in search of breathtaking itineraries, fresh horizons carved by Nature, and daring, seemingly impossible ascents. Their entry on the scientific scene and indeed their name date back to 1788, when their geological composition was determined by Déodat de Dolomieu. Our journey, then, will be imbued with the spirit of the travellers of old, in which dreams vied with reality in an aura of mystery and fascination. From the pastures that encircle the Costalunga Pass, the red face of the Roda di Vaèl, which stands in the Southern part of the Catinaccio Group, provides us with a symbolic introduction to the world of rocks and light of what were once known as »The Pale Mountains«.

2. ZWÖLFERKOFEL (3094 m) — EINSERKOFEL (2696 m) — DREISCHUSTERSPITZE (3145 m)

◀ 0 |45° |90° |135° |180° |200° |220° |240°

3. DREISCHUSTERSPITZE (3145 m) — KLEINSCHUSTERSPITZE (3095 m) — WIENERTURM (2892 m)

4.

Vom Fischleinboden aus, wo die Straße durch das Sextental endet, erblickt man genau im Zentrum den wunderschönen Komplex des Zwölferkofels (3094 m), der das Fischleintal beherrscht (Bild 2). Zur Linken ist der Elferkofel (3029 m) zu sehen, dessen Flanke auf halber Höhe der historische Alpini-Weg (»strada degli Alpini«) zum Sentinella-Paß durchzieht, einem Kampfplatz des Ersten Weltkriegs. Rechts ragt die Nordwand des Einserkofels empor, die Angelo Dibona aus Cortina und Luigi Rizzi aus Fassa 1910 in direktem Anstieg bezwungen haben. Rechts, fast verdeckt, erscheint der gezackte Gipfel der Dreischusterspitze (3145 m). Wir befinden uns hier im Herzen der Sextener Dolomiten, dem äußersten nordöstlichen Teil der Südtiroler Dolomiten, in einer Umgebung, die der hohen Zahl von Ausflüglern und Bergsteigern zum Trotz ihre Schönheit und ihre landschaftliche

From Campo Fiscalino at the end of the road running through the Sesto Valley, one's eye is struck by the wonderful complex of Zwölferkofel (3094 m) in the centre, overlooking Val Fiscalina (No. 2). On the left, there is the Elfer (3092 m), crossed at mid-height by the ledge that forms the »Strada degli Alpini«, the well-known route leading to the Sentinella Pass of first world war fame and memory. The North face of Einser can be seen on the right. The direct route up this bulwark was pioneered by two guides, Angelo Dibona from Cortina and Luigi Rizzi from the Fassa Valley, in 1910. Further to the right is the jagged summit of the Dreischusterspitze (3145 m). This is the heart of the Sesto section of the Dolomites, i. e. the furthermost North-Eastern part of the Trentino Alto Adige Region (Sud-Tirol). Despite its great popularity with hikers and climbers, it has retained its particular beauty and kept its

Unberührtheit erhalten konnte. Die ganze Region, zu der auch die Drei Zinnen gehören, liegt im Nationalpark Sextener Dolomiten. Die Dreischusterspitze beherrscht mit ihrer Gipfelkrone das bezaubernde Innerfeldtal. Auf der rechten Seite erheben sich Kleinschusterspitze (3095 m) und Wienerturm (2892 m) mit der Schusterscharte und links dem Steinalpenkar. Die Erstbesteigung der Dreischusterspitze gelang 1869 dem Wiener Paul Grohmann und den Bergführern Franz Innerkofler und Peter Salcher. Unter den Gipfeln der Sextener Dolomiten nimmt diese Gruppe einen besonderen Platz ein, und der Blick vom Innerfeldtal ist ohne Zweifel einer der eindrucksvollsten und bezauberndsten. Die einsame Kapelle von Fodara Vedla, in einer typischen Frühlingsstimmung (Bild 4). Neben Anstiegen jeglichen Schwierigkeitsgrads bietet die Dolomitenlandschaft zahlreiche Möglichkeiten, die Schönheit ihrer verschiedenen Jahreszeiten zu genießen.

landscape intact. The whole area, in fact, including the renowned Tre Cime di Lavaredo, lies within the Dolomiti di Sesto Nature Reserve. The peaks of the Dreischusterspitze (No. 3) overlook the enchanting Val Campodidentro. On the right, the Kleiner Schuster (3095 m), and the Wienerturm (2892 m) with the Schusterscharte gully; on the left, the Steinalpenkar. The Dreischusterspitze was first climbed in 1869 by the Viennese Alpinist Paul Grohmann and two guides, Franz Innerkofler and Peter Salcher. This group is readily recognizable from the floor of the Sesto Valley. The view from Val Campodidentro is certainly the most impressive. The solitary Fodara Vedla Chapel (No. 4) in a typical springtime setting. In addition to climbs of varying degrees of difficulty, the Dolomites offer both walkers and hikers innumerable opportunities to enjoy the beauties of their different seasons.

5.

Wenn man das Pragser Tal durchwandert — es ist einer der schönsten Winkel in den Südtiroler Dolomiten — gelangt man an das südliche Ufer des gleichnamigen Sees. Wir befinden uns in den Pragser Dolomiten, die eine einzigartige geomorphologische Struktur aufweisen; im Norden reichen sie bis zum Pustertal, im Osten grenzen die Sextener Dolomiten an und im Süden die Cristallogruppe. Von den Ufern des Pragser Wildsees erhebt sich über mehr als 1000 Meter hoch der Gran Sàss dla Porta (2810 m); diesen Namen haben die ladinischen Bewohner des Ennebergtals dem Seekofel gegeben. Die Pragser Dolomiten machen einen großen Teil des Naturparks Fanes — Sennes — Prags aus.

Val di Bràies is one of the most enchanting corners of the South Tyrolean Dolomites. This section of the mountains is bounded on the North by Val Pusteria, on the East by the Dolomiti di Sesto, and on the South by the Gruppo di Cristallo, and displays unusual geomorphological features. The solitary peak of the Seekofel (2810 m) — known to the Ladin inhabitants of Val di Marebbe as Gran Sass dla Porta — rises for over 1000 metres above the shores of Lake Bràies at the head of the valley in a very varied setting. The Bràies Dolomites make up a substantial part of the Fanes-Sennes-Bràies Nature Reserve.

6.

In den Ampezzaner Dolomiten erheben sich vor dem Sorapis (3205 m) rechts, in Wolken eingehüllt, die Monti della Cacciagrande, die den großen, einzigartigen und wilden Gletscherzirkus beherrschen. Links, vom Val di San Vito abgeschnitten, spitzen einige Gipfel der Marmarolegruppe hervor. Das umfangreiche Bergmassiv des Sorapis ist durch seine mächtige, 2000 Meter hohe Wand, die gegen Westen abfällt, unverwechselbar. Die lange Marmarole-Kette besteht aus Gipfeln von fast gleicher Höhe, die immer Spuren von Schnee tragen. Wenn man die Marmarole-Berge in ihrer komplexen Gliederung betrachtet, erscheinen sie unbezwingbar: eine geheimnisvolle und unwegsame Gruppe, die zu vielen Sagen angeregt hat.

In the Ampezzo section of the Dolomites, Punta di Sorapis (3205 m), hidden in the clouds on the right, is preceded by the Monti della Cacciagrande overlooking a wild, grandiose glacial cirque. On the left, divided by Val di San Vito, some peaks of the Gruppo delle Marmarole stand out. A distinctive feature of the extensive Sorapis massif is the mighty 2000-metre face that falls away to the West. The long chain known as the Marmarole consists of peaks that are nearly all of the same height and never without some patches of snow. Their complex interweaving makes them seem inaccessible, and this mysterious, impenetrable group has not surprisingly been the source of many legends in the ancient lore of the Dolomites.

7.

8.

CRISTALLINO (2775 m)

PIZ POPENA (3152 m)

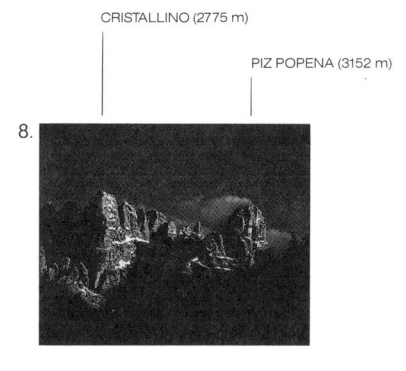

Der Cristallo (3221 m) in den Ampezzaner Dolomiten spiegelt sich im dunklen Wasser des Dürrensees (Bild 7). Tiefe Abgründe und gerundete Gipfelgrate bestimmen sein Profil, das sich nach der zum See hin gelegenen Seite mit großer Feierlichkeit zeigt. Von wo aus man ihn auch betrachtet, sein Aufbau, die Farbe seiner Felsen und sein abwechslungsreiches Aussehen sind ein Beispiel für reinen Dolomit. Der Cristallo-Paß trennt ihn vom Piz Popena, gefolgt von einigen Spitzen des Cristallino di Misurina. Die Nordwand des Monte Cristallo wurde 1877 von Michael Innerkofler, einem Führer aus Sexten, bezwungen. Innerkofler wird die Besteigung dieser Felsenbastion noch gut 300mal wiederholen, bevor er dabei schließlich im August 1888 den Tod finden wird. Die letzten Strahlen der untergehenden Sonne beleuchten die Felsnadeln und Grate, die, vom Cristallino di Misurina (2775 m) ausgehend, zum Piz Popena hinführen (Bild 8).

Monte Cristallo (3221 m), another component of the Ampezzo Dolomites, stands out from the other peaks as it gazes at its reflection in the waters of the Dürrensee. Its profile is marked by high precipices and peaks with rounded edges, and creates a solemn atmosphere on this side. The mountain itself is a fine example of true dolomite when seen from any angle, as can be judged from its formation, the colour of its rocks, and its variegated appearance. The Passo del Cristallo divides it from Piz Popena, which is followed by the heights of the Cristallino di Misurina. The North face of the Cristallino was first climbed in 1877 by Michael Innerkofler, a guide from Sesto, who went on reach the top a full 300 times before losing his life on this same mountain in August 1888. The last rays of the setting sun light up the pinnacles and spires of the Cristallino di Misurina (2775 m) (No. 8) as they run off to join Piz Popena (3152 m).

9.

Die Bergalm wird oft als Modell eines vielseitig verwendbaren ländlichen Gebäudes herangezogen: sie mußte einen effektiven Kompromiß zwischen den Wohnbedürfnissen der Menschen und den der Arbeit in Land- und Almwirtschaft finden. Ein großer Holzofen, häufig im hellsten Teil des Gebäudes eingebaut, bestimmte die weitere Raumaufteilung im Inneren der Hütte. Hochmittelalterliche Baumodelle finden ebenso wie die altbewährten Baumaterialien auch heute noch Anwendung.

The mountain-dweller's malga is often cited as a model of a multipurpose rural edifice. Its aim was to find an effective compromise between a dwelling in the usual sense and a place catering for the needs of those engaged in growing crops and pasturing livestock. The large wood oven, often set in the best-lit corner, is one of the features that determined the layout of the interior. Patterns first conceived in the early Middle Ages and modified over the centuries are still used today, and the same materials are naturally employed.

10.

11.

Die Croda Marcora (3154 m) im Boite-Tal über der Ortschaft San Vito di Cadore ist die schönste, da offenste und sonnigste Dolomitenwand (Bild 10). Die Croda, eigentlich die Südwand des Sorapis, wurde von den Talbewohnern Marcora getauft, weil die Sonne an ihr den ganzen Tag über die Zeit angibt (»marca l'ora«). Wir sind im Herzen der Östlichen Dolomiten, einem Land mit Gipfeln der Superlative, die wegen ihrer Stattlichkeit zu den wichtigsten des dolomitischen Bogens ernannt wurden. Die Landschaft, die durch diese Felskolosse geprägt wird, öffnet sich zu Aussichten seltener Schönheit, die die Ortschaften in den Tälern um Cadore hervorheben. Der Kirchturm von Borca di Cadore (Bild 11) scheint sich hier mit dem mächtigen Profil des Monte Pelmo zu unterhalten.

The Croda Marcora (3154 m) rises above San Vito di Cadore in the Bòite Valley and is the finest, sunniest and most open face of the Dolomites. Baptised in this way by the valley dwellers because the sun »marks the hour« on its surface all day, it is really the South-West of the Sorapis in the Eastern Dolomites, whose superlative peaks are often put forward as the main features of the Dolomites as a whole because they are so impressive. The natural landscape formed by these tall peaks is etched with unusually attractive corners that provided an enchanting background to the town and villages of the Cadore valleys. The backlit campanile of the church of Borca di Cadore (No. 11) seems to wish to share confidence with Monte Pelmo.

12.

13.

PELMO (3169 m)

PELMETTO (2993 m)

Die Kirchen von Santa Fosca im Fiorentina-Tal (Bild 12) mit der Marmolada im Hintergrund und eine Ansicht der isoliert stehenden Pelmogruppe (3169 m) in den Zoldiner Dolomiten, aufgenommen von Nordwesten, mit dem Hauptgipfel auf der linken Seite; rechts der Pelmetto (2993 m). Die zwischen Antelao und Civetta gelegene Gruppe ragt über den Tälern von Boite und Zoldo auf. Es ist interessant zu wissen, daß der in Pieve del Cadore geborene Maler Tizian eine detaillierte Zeichnung von diesem Berg angefertigt hat. Der Pelmo ist ein Naturmonument von wirklich atemberaubender Schönheit. Er wurde bereits 1857 bezwungen, und zwar von dem englischen Wissenschaftler und Bergsteiger John Ball, der bis unter den Hauptgipfel von einem Gemsenjäger begleitet wurde. Erst 1924 gelang es Roland Rossi und Felix Simon in direktem Anstieg die gefürchtete Nordwand von fast 1000 Meter Höhe zu überwinden. Auch heute noch gilt diese Route als eine der schwierigsten der Dolomiten.

The church of Santa Fosca, Val Fiorentina (No. 12), with the Marmolada massif in the background, and a view of the isolated Gruppo del Pelmo (3169 m) in the Zoldo Dolomites taken from the North-West with the Cime della Val D'Arcia on the left, and the Pelmetto or Lesser Pelmo (2993 m) on the right. This group lies between the Antelao and the Civetta. It overlooks the Boìte and Zoldo Valleys and one of its main features is the two separate blocks of the Fessura (2726 m). The word Pelmo was the local pre-Roman name for rock. A detailed drawing of this mountain was made by Tizian, who was born at Pieve del Cadore. The Pelmo is indeed a natural monument to be viewed with bated breath. It was the first of the Dolomites to be climbed. Its conqueror was the British scientist John Ball, who was accompanied to just below the main peak by a chamois hunter. It was not until 1924 that the North face — a sheer drop of nearly 1000 metres — was scaled by Roland Rossi and Felix Simon. This direct route is still one of the most taxing in the Dolomites.

14.

Eine der Berghütten, die das Dorf Fodàra Vedla (ladinisch: Alte Kaseralm) zu Füßen der legendären Crode di Larinòres bilden. Fodàra Vedla ist eine Fortsetzung der Sennesalpe in den Dolomiten um Enneberg. Auch wenn man den Eindruck bekommt, ein Dorf vor sich zu haben, handelt es sich tatsächlich nur um eine Anzahl von Hütten, die für die Weidewirtschaft genutzt werden. Die von der Almwirtschaft geprägten Bräuche ähneln auch heute noch stark denen der vor 1000 Jahren eingewanderten Siedler, die sich in dieser Talebene niedergelassen haben. Die wirtschaftliche und soziale Isoliertheit war die Grundbedingung dafür, daß sich hier sehr urtümliche Arbeits- und Lebensgewohnheiten erhalten konnten.

One of the baite (»chalets«) that make up the village of Fodàra Vedla (Ladin: »old mountain dairy hut«) at the feet of the renowned Crode di Lavinòres. This village is an offshoot of Alpe di Sennes in the Marebbe Dolomites. Set in a green cirque surrounded by pastures and watered by the Fodàra, it is really more of collection of malghe devoted to the tasks associated with the pasturing of herds, since these are still very much in tune with the ways practised by the peoples who colonised these valleys a thousand years ago. The social and economic isolation throughout the centuries helped to preserve ancient ways of live and work.

15.

Die Ruine des Castello di Andràz (1774 m), auf halber Höhe des Col di Lana in der Nähe von Livinallongo gelegen, bietet ein klassisches Bild der Dolomitenlandschaft, indem sich die Zinnen der Berge in denen der Burg wiederfinden. Die Befestigungsanlage steht auf einem Felsblock von außerordentlicher Größe. Die strategisch günstige Lage und die eindeutige Bauweise als Bollwerk lassen die enormen Verteidigungsmöglichkeiten des Bauwerks erkennen. Es wurde wahrscheinlich um das 11. Jahrhundert, einige Jahrzehnte nach der Gründung der bischöflichen Herrschaft in Brixen, errichtet.

The ruins of Andràz Castle (1774 m) near Livinallongo on the waist of the green cupola of the Col di Lana offer a classic illustration of the Dolomitic landscape, be it solely for their resemblance to the surrounding peaks. The castle occupied the whole summit of an exceptionally massive knoll and in this respect clearly resembles Hauenstein Castle on the Siusi Plateau. It was probably built around the 11th century, a few decades after the establishment of the Episcopal Principate of Bressanone. Its strategic position and its evident creation as a bulwark suggest that it was readily defensible.

Soraga di Fassa, eine kleine Stadt im gleichnamigen Tal, liegt im ladinischen Teil des Trentino, überragt vom grünen Rücken des Ciampedie und den Wänden von Larséch, einer südöstlichen Untergruppe des Rosengartens (Bild 16). Der Scalette-Paß teilt die steilen Wände von Larséch, rechts zeichnet sich der schlanke und spitze Torre Rizzi (2485 m) ab, der 1899 von Luigi Rizzi, Luigi Bernard und Emilia Plank erstbestiegen wurde. Von der Aussichtskanzel der Pordoispitze (2950 m; Bild 17) tut sich ein nahezu vollständiger Blick auf die Dolomiten und auf das benachbarte Gebirge auf. Rechts der Kamm des Piz Ciavazes (2828 m), der aus dem Sellastock emporragt. Das Panorama zeigt die Langkofelgruppe mit der im Schatten liegenden grandiosen Nordwand des Hauptgipfels; links, über den Hängen des Sellajochs, taucht die wuchtige Pyramide der Grohmannspitze (3124 m) auf. Sie erhielt diesen Namen zu Ehren Paul Grohmanns, einem Wiener Bergsteiger, der als erster Marmolada und Langkofel bezwungen hatte. Der Sellastock wird eingegrenzt vom Grödner Joch, dem Sellajoch, dem Pordoijoch und dem Campolongo-Paß.

Soraga di Fassa, a small town in the valley of the same name, lies in the Ladin part of the Trentino below the green ridge of the Ciampedie and the Dirupi di Larséch, a South-Eastern sub-group of the Rosengarten (No. 16). The Scalette Pass divides the crags from the Dirupi. On the right, there is the slender Rizzi Tower (2485 m), climbed for the first time in 1898 by Luigi Rizzi, Luigi Bernard and Emilia Plank. From the balcony of Sass Pordoi (2950 m; No. 17) one of the most complete views can be had of the Dolomites and their neighbours. On the right, the ridge of Piz Ciavàzes (2828 m) rising from the large middle terrace of the Sella Group. The panorama proceeds as far as the Langkofel Group, where the grandiose wall of the main peak can be discerned in the shade, while to the left, above the slopes of the Sella Pass, there is the great pyramid named Grohmannspitze (3124 m) in honour of Paul Grohmann, the Viennese climber who first set foot on the summits of the Marmolada and the Langkofel. The Sella Group comprises four interlinked passes — Gardena, Sella, Pordoi and Campolungo.

SCHARTENTURM (2660 m)
VAJOLETNADEL (2710 m)
NORDTURM (2810 m)
DELAGOTURM (2790 m)
PIAZTURM (2760 m)

ROTWAND (2806 m)
TEUFELSWAND (2723 m)

20.

21.

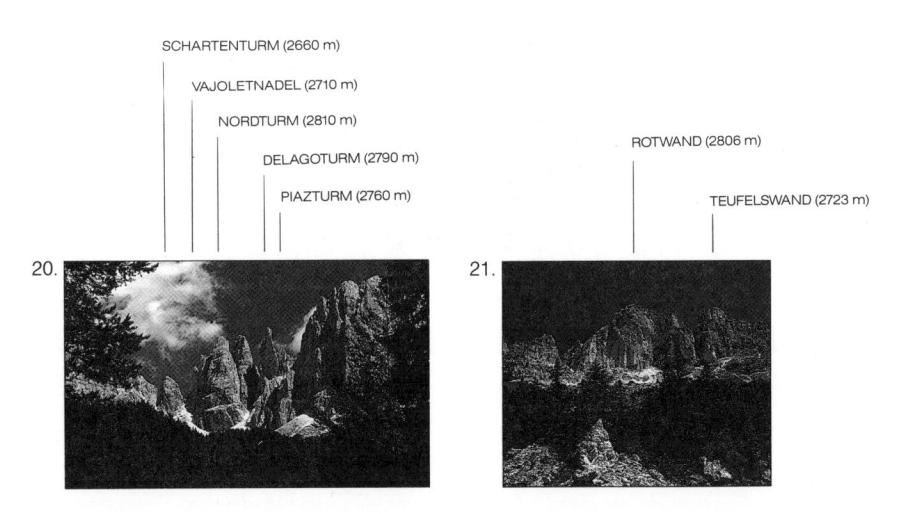

Der Karersee (1530 m) spiegelt in seinem Wasser die bekannte Bergkette des Latemar (Bild 18) wieder. Der See und die Wände, die seinen Rahmen bilden, bezeichnen einen der einprägsamsten Winkel der Südtiroler Dolomiten. Hinter den Hauptgipfeln von Cornón und Schenón, gefolgt von der Großen Scharte, erheben sich der Christomannosturm, der Cimón del Latemàr und die Westlichen Türme. Die Ansammlung von Gipfeln im Vordergrund verstellt jedoch den Blick auf eine Vielzahl von weiteren Türmen und Felsnadeln — eine Welt, die für jene unsichtbar bleibt, die sich nicht mit den Wegen durch diese geheimnisvolle und zerklüftete Gruppe vertraut machen. Der Nigerpaß (Bild 19) wird zur Linken von den Wänden der östlichen Rosengartengruppe gesäumt; er bildet einen befahrbaren Übergang zwischen dem Tierser Tal und dem Karerpaß. Im Zentrum liegt noch der Latemar, gefolgt von den grünen Gipfeln der Rocca und dem Weißhorn. Auf der Seite des Tierstals, in der Nähe der Costa-Alm, zeigt der Rosengarten eines seiner unverkennbaren Profile (Bild 20). Von links erblickt man den Schartenturm (2660 m), dann folgen die Große Scharte (2580 m) und die Vajolettürme: Vajoletnadel (2710 m), Nordturm (2810 m), Delago (2790 m) und Piazturm (2670 m). Der folgende Einschnitt des Laurinspaß wird von der gleichnamigen Wand beherrscht. Der Hauptturm (2821 m), höchster der nördlichen Vajolettürme, liegt neben dem berühmten Winklerturm (2800 m). Er wurde im August 1882 von den Kletterern Giambattista Bernard und Gottfried Merzbacher erstmals bezwungen; diese leiteten damit die Erstbesteigungen der anderen Türme ein. Um die Rosengartengruppe ranken sich die schönsten Sagen und Legenden der Dolomitenwelt mit ihrer phantastischen Figur des König Laurin und seinem wunderbaren, in Stein verwandelten Rosengarten. Hier erzeugt das warme Licht der letzten Sonnenstrahlen den bewegenden Augenblick des Alpenglühens; dann nehmen Felsen, Felsnadeln, Gipfel und Türme die allerschönsten Rottöne an, gleich den Rosen im Garten des gutmütigen Königs, der mit seinen Zwergen dieses Gebirge bewohnte. Im letzten Bild (Bild 21) ist die Rotwand (2806 m) mit dem Vajolonpaß und dem Vajolonkopf zur Linken zu sehen; rechts der Fensterlturm und die Teufelswand (2723 m).

The Karer See (1530 m). The Northern chain of the Latemàr (2842 m) is reflected in its waters (No. 18). This lake and the mountain faces that form its frame constitute one of the most enticing corners of the South Tyrolean Dolomites. The limpidity of the water is such as to wash away, as if by magic, any difference between the real mountain and its reflection. Behind the main peaks of Cornón and Schenón, followed by Forcella Grande, the Cristomannos Tower, the Cimón del Latemàr, and the Western Towers stand out. Yet the curtain of peaks forming the foreground of our photo itself masks a multitude of towers and needles, a world invisible to all but those who venture into the byways of this mysterious, haunted group. The Niger Pass (No. 19), a road crossing between the Costalunga Pass and the Tires Valley, is overlooked on the left by the faces of the Eastern sector of the Rosengarten Group. In the centre once again is the Latemàr massif followed by the green mounds of the Rocca and the Corno Bianco. On the Tires Valley side, near Malga Costa (2660 m), the Rosengarten offers one of its unmistakable profiles. From left to right, we have the Del Passo Tower (2660 m), followed by the Forcella Grande (2580 m) and the Vaiolét Towers: Estrema (2710 m), Nord (2810 m), Delago (2790 m) and Piaz (2670 m). The next notch — the Laurins Pass — lies below the crag bearing its name. The Main Tower (2821 m), the highest of the Vaiolèt's Northern set and beside the renowned Winkler Tower (2800 m), was conquered in August 1882 by Giambattista Bernard and Gottfried Merzbacher, the first of the series of exploits that took climbers to the top of the other towers. The Rosengarten Group is associated with the Dolomites' finest sagas and legends, woven around the fanciful figure of King Laurin and his marvellous rose garden transformed into stone. When the sun's dying rays provide the magic moment known as the alpenglow, these ridges, needles, peaks and towers are bathed in the finest shades of red, just like the roses in the garden of this kindhearted monarch, who once dwelt in these mountains with his dwarves. The last photo (No. 21) shows us the Roda di Vaèl (2806 m) with the Vaiolón Pass and the Testone del Vaiolón on the left, and the Forcella delle Rode and the Roda del Diavolo (2723 m) on the right.

WASSERKOFEL (2924 m)
ODLA DI VALDUSSA (2936 m)
FURCHETTA (3025 m)
SASS RIGAIS (3025 m)
CUMEDEL (2755 m)
ODLA DI FUNES (2800 m)
CAMPANILE DI FUNES (2840 m)
GROSSE FERMEDA (2873 m)
KLEINE FERMEDA (2814 m)

22.

23.

Die Geislerspitzen (Bild 22) von Norden mit den Wiesen der Zannseralm im Villnößtal im Vordergrund. Die Aufnahme zeigt den für die Dolomiten so typischen Kontrast zwischen Felswänden und großen Grünflächen mit Wiesen und Weiden. Die Geislergruppe, die das Villnößtal vom Grödnertal trennt, weist eine ganze Schar von Felsnadeln und von hohen, schmalen Graten auf. Von links nach rechts kann man erkennen: Wasserkofel (2924 m), Odla di Valdussa (2936 m), Furchetta (3025 m) und Sass Rigais (3025 m). Nach der Mittagsscharte geht es weiter mit Cumedèl (2755 m), Odla di Funes (2800 m), dem Campanile di Funes (2840 m), der Großen Fermeda (2873 m) und der Kleinen Fermeda (2814 m). Die erste Besteigung der Geislerspitzen gelang dem Südtiroler Kletterer Johann Santner, der im September 1880 den Gipfel der Furchetta über die Südwand erklomm. Die Nordwand der Furchetta, die der auffälligste Gipfel der Gruppe ist, wurde einst als einer der schwierigsten Anstiege der gesamten Dolomiten klassifiziert. Erst 1925 wurde sie von dem berühmten deutschen Bergführer Emil Solleder in Begleitung von Franz Wiesner durchstiegen. Vom Würzjoch aus (Bild 23) zeigt sich die Nordseite des Peitlerkofels (2875 m) in ihrer ganzen Stattlichkeit.

The Odle Group (No. 22) taken from the North side, with the meadows of Malga Zànnes in Val di Funes in the foreground. A picture that illustrates the happy contrast between rocky faces and large patches of meadows and pastures which is often encountered in the Dolomites. This Group separates Val Gardena from the Valle di Funes. The word »odla« means a needle and is here most appropriately applied to the Group's striking array of peaks: from left to right, Sàss da l'Ega (2924 m), Odla di Valdussa (2936 m), Furchetta (3025 m), and sàss Rigàis (3025 m). Then the Forcella di Mesdì is followed by the Cumedèl (2755 m), Odla di Funes (2800 m), the Campanile di Funes (2840 m), and the Grande and Little Fermeda (2873 and 2814 m). The first recorded ascent of the Odle is that of the Alto-Adigean climber Johann Santner, who reached the summit of the Furchetta via the South face in September 1880. The North face was initially regarded as one of the most tricky climbs in the Dolomites. Indeed, it was not conquered until 1925 by the famous German guide Emil Solleder, accompanied by Franz Weissener. The imposing North side of Sàss de Pütia (2875 m) can be seen from the Delle Erbe Pass (No. 23).

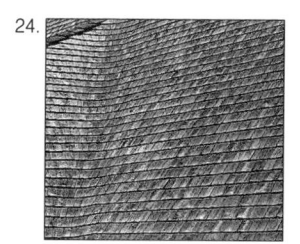

24.

Das gleichmäßige Gewebe einer althergebrachten Dachhaut aus Lärchenschindeln, dem für die Dolomitenregion typischen Material zum Dachdecken. Die Eigenheiten und Charakteristika der Bauweise in den Bergen sind das Ergebnis von jahrhundertealten Erfahrungen im Umgang mit dem örtlich vorhandenen Baumaterial. Die holzverarbeitende Bautechnik ist traditionsreich und in den gesamten Dolomiten anzutreffen; sie ist ästhetisch wie technisch sehr ausgefeilt. Die Dachschindeln aus Lärche werden in doppelter Schicht und regelmäßigen Bahnen am Dachstuhl befestigt. Dichtere Reihen im Hauptteil — typische Eigenschaft einiger kleiner Kunstbauten in den ladinischen Tälern — machen die Befestigung der Dachhäute mit Steinen unnötig. Obwohl es in der Vergangenheit nicht an negativen Gegenbeispielen gefehlt hat, stellt der gute Erhaltungszustand der Siedlungen in der ganzen Dolomitenregion zusammen mit der Landschaft eine Art »Beweisstück« und eine reiche Informationsquelle zum kulturellen Erbe dar.

The regular texture of a classic mantle of larch tiles, the typical material used to finish buildings in the Dolomites. The characteristic features of mountain architecture have been devised over the centuries and stem from the requirements imposed by such materials as are available locally. Wood can be found at any point throughout the Alps and is often used to obtain both attractive and technically impressive results. The larch tiles installed on usually double-pitch roofs are laid in uniform rows and attached to the structure. Thicker rows in the middle — a feature of some buildings in the Ladin valleys — make it unnecessary to employ stones to hold the mantle in place. Notwithstanding some instances to the contrary in the past, the good level of preservation of the habitations in the Dolomites confers the status of a »record« on the landscape, making it a source of information on the local culture.

25.

Cortina, die »Königin der Dolomiten«. Das Szenario der Berge, die das Talbecken von Cortina umgeben, ist außerordentlich: Monte Cristallo, Tofana, Sorapis und Antelao. Der Wiener Paul Grohmann, der vieles über die Berge um Cortina geschrieben hat, bezeichnete die Stadt als das »Mekka der Dolomiten«, als den Ort, wohin jeder unweigerlich zurückkehren muß, der diese Berge liebt. Schon im letzten Jahrhundert profitierte Cortina als Hauptort an der Großen Dolomitenstraße von der zunehmenden Zahl englischer und deutscher Bergsteiger. Dieser erste Impuls brachte einen Sommer- und Wintertourismus auf hohem Niveau in Gang, der ab den zwanziger Jahren unseres Jahrhunderts aus Cortina ein mondänes Touristen- und Sportzentrum von internationalem Ruf machte.

Cortina, »Queen of the Dolomites«. The cirque in which it stands is indeed surrounded by wondrous mountains: Cristallo, Tofane, Sorapis, Antelào, This »Mecca of the Dolomites«, as it was described Paul Grohmann, of whom we have already heard tell (No. 17) and who here wrote some of Alpinism's noblest pages, this place to which those who love the mountains must inevitably return, earned fame and fortune even in the 19th century owing to its assiduous frequentation by both British and German climbers. This initial impetus was such that Cortina, a keypoint along the Great Dolomites Highway and endowed with an incomparably attractive setting, blossomed out to receive the cream of both summer and winter tourists, so that its fame as a fashionable resort made it a household word by the Twenties.

26.

MONTE AVERAU (2649 m)
NUVOLAU (2574 m)
RA GUSÈLA (2595 m)

Teilansicht der Tofana di Rozes (Bild 26) inmitten des beeindruckenden Bergkomplexes, der die Westseite des Ampezzaner Beckens abschließt. Die drei Tofanagipfel sind über 3000 Meter hoch. Ist die Tofana di Mezzo (3243 m) auch die höchste, so gilt die mächtige Tofana di Rozes (3223 m) mit Sicherheit unter Bergsteigern als die begehrteste. Auf dem folgenden Bild (Bild 27) ein Blick vom Passo di Giau auf das Zentrum der Ampezzaner Dolomiten mit dem bedrohlich erscheinenden Ra Gusèla (2595 m), der über einen langen Grat mit dem Nuvolau (2574 m) verbunden ist. Links der Monte Averau (2649 m). Auf dem letzten Bild (Bild 28) das Talbecken von Cortina d'Ampezzo in einem Rundumblick von 360 Grad: links die Gipfel des Pomagagnon und der Monte Cristallo, eingehüllt in Wolken, die seinem Gipfel eine Krone aufsetzen. Nach dem Tre-Croci-Paß, einem der eindrucksvollsten Übergänge zum Ampezzaner Talbecken, erheben sich der Faloria mit der Sorapisgruppe und rechts der Antelao, höchster Gipfel in den Östlichen Dolomiten. Außer dem Val del Boite beschließen die Rocchetta mit dem Becco di Mezzodi, die Croda da Lago und der waldreiche Pocol den Rundblick; es folgt die über den Col Druscie hinausragende Tofanagruppe.

A detail of Tofana di Rozes (3223 m), the middle of three peaks — all over 3000 metres — that seal in the Western end of the Ampezzo basin. The highest is Tofana di Mezzo (3243 m), whereas Tofana di Rozes is the most panoramic and certainly the one that enjoys pride of place in the eyes of climbers. Photo No. 27 offers a view of the Giau Pass at the centre of the Ampezzo Dolomites, together with Ra Gusèla (2595 m), connected by a long ridge to the Nuvolau (2574 m). Monte Averau (2649 m) can be seen on the left. The last of these three pictures is a 360° panorama of the bowl in which Cortina lies: from left to right, the peaks forming the Pomagagnón, and the Cristallo, whose summit is wreathed in clouds. Next comes the Tre Croci Pass, the most attractive passage through the centre of the Ampezzano region, then the Falòria with the Soràpis Group, and on the right the Antelào (3264 m), the highest peak in the Eastern Dolomites. Beyond Val del Bòite, our »circumspection« comes to a close with the Rocchetta, the Becco di Mezzodi, the Croda da Lago, the forest-girt Pocol, and the Tofane Group overlooking Col Drusciè.

Die Cinque Torri, gigantische Felsblöcke in der Nuvolaugruppe, im Süden an der Großen Dolomitenstraße zwischen Falzaregopaß und Cortina gelegen. Der Gipfel des Nuvolau (2574 m), der meistbestiegene der Gruppe, spielt innerhalb dieser unglaublichen Naturerscheinungen eher eine Nebenrolle. Die tief zerklüfteten Felstürme bereichern die eindrucksvolle Silhouette dieses natürlichen Felspalastes, an dem Generationen von Bergsteigern ihr Kletterkönnen unter Beweis gestellt haben. Der Torre Grande (2366 m), dessen Wand mehr als 160 Meter steil aufragt, wurde 1880 zum ersten Mal erreicht, und zwar von C. G. Wall mit dem Führer Giuseppe Ghedina aus Cortina. Die anderen Türme — normalerweise der Reihe nach aufgezählt vom Zweiten zum Fünften — werden auch Torre Romana, Torre Latina, Torre Andrea und Torre Inglese genannt. Von Osten aus erscheint der Zweite Turm als ein einheitlicher Block, er setzt sich aber in Wirklichkeit aus den Türmen Barancio und Lusy zusammen. Die Türme werden von Bergsteigern das ganze Jahr über als Klettergarten genutzt.

The Cinque Torri (Five Towers), gigantic blocks of dolomite, in the Nuvolau Group to the South of the road from the Falzarego Pass to Cortina. Nuvolau itself (2574 m), the most heavily-trodden member of the Group, is almost rendered of secondary importance by this incredible example of Nature's creative hand. Enormous cracks enhance the intriguing silhouette of this natural rock-climber's proving-ground, where generations of mountaineers have put their technical skills and practical abilities to the test. The Torre Grande (2366 m), whose sheer wall rises for more than 160 metres, was climbed for the first time in 1880 by C. G. Wall in the company of Giuseppe Ghedina, a guide from Cortina. The other Towers (usually known as the Second to the Fifth) are also called the Torre Romana, the Torre Latina, the Torre Andrea, and the Torre Inglese. When seen from the East, the Second Tower appears to be a single piece, whereas in fact it also comprises the Barancio and the Lusy Towers. Often used as training grounds, these Towers can be scaled the whole year round and offer the climber a wide range of alternatives.

Die Furcia dai Fers (2532 m) auf der Fanesalpe in den Dolomiten um Enneberg. Das Gebiet von Fanes und Sennes im Südtiroler Raum ist das Zentrum des gleichnamigen Naturparks. In diesem Abschnitt der Nördlichen Dolomiten, zwischen Enneberg und dem Dürrensee, erstreckt sich auch das Gebiet, das in dem wunderbaren Sagenzyklus, den uns der Schriftsteller Karl Felix Wolff übermittelt hat, eine besondere Rolle spielt. Hier nämlich erstreckte sich das mythische Land von Fanes, einem mächtigen Gebirgsherrscher, der reich an Ländereien und Äckern war. Das Schloß, in dem der König dieses sagenumwobenen Volkes lebte, befand sich im südlichen Teil des Conturines. Die Fanes, auch Marmotten oder Murmeltiere genannt, waren ein gutmütiges und ängstliches Volk; so ängstlich, daß sie sich vor Feinden in den Felsschluchten versteckten. Aber die Sage erzählt auch, daß ihr letzter König ein tüchtiger Krieger war, der mit seinen Eroberungen das Land noch größer und reicher machte. Dann kamen jedoch andere Völker, die mit der Unterdrückung des Volkes von Fanes deren Herrschaft endgültig zerstörten. Der Pragser Wildsee, in dem sich der gewaltige Seekofel (auf ladinisch Sàss dla Porta) spiegelt, verbirgt den letzten geheimnisvollen Wohnsitz der Fanes.

The Furcia dai Fers (2532 m) in the Alpe di Fànes stands in the Marebbe Dolomites. The Fànes and Sennes area forms part of the Alto Adige and is the centre of a nature reserve bearing the same name. Here, in this sector of the Northern Dolomites between Marebbe and the Dürrensee, is the strip of country whose name is linked to the wondrous cycle of legends handed down by the writer Karl Felix Wolff. Here, in fact, was the mythical land of Fànes, a splendid mountain kingdom, abounding in towns and fields. The castle, where the king of this legendary people dwelt, lay in the Southern part of the Conturines. The Fànes folk were kind and shy. Known as the »Marmots«, they were so afraid of enemies that they would hide in the crannies of the rocks to avoid them. Yet the legend has it that their last king was a valiant warrior, whose conquests made his realm even larger and richer. Other peoples came, however, Overthrew the local inhabitants and destroyed the kingdom. Lake Bràies, whose waters reflect the mighty Seekofel, which the Ladins call the Sàss dla Porta, hides the last mysterious refuge of the Fànes, an underground region protected by the roots of the mountain.

32.

CRODA DEL RIFUGIO
IL MULO
CRODA DEGLI ALPINI
WESTLICHE ZINNE (2973 m)
GROSSE ZINNE (2999 m)
KLEINE ZINNE (2856 m)
PUNTA DI FRIDA (2785 m)
KLEINSTE ZINNE (2700 m)

33.

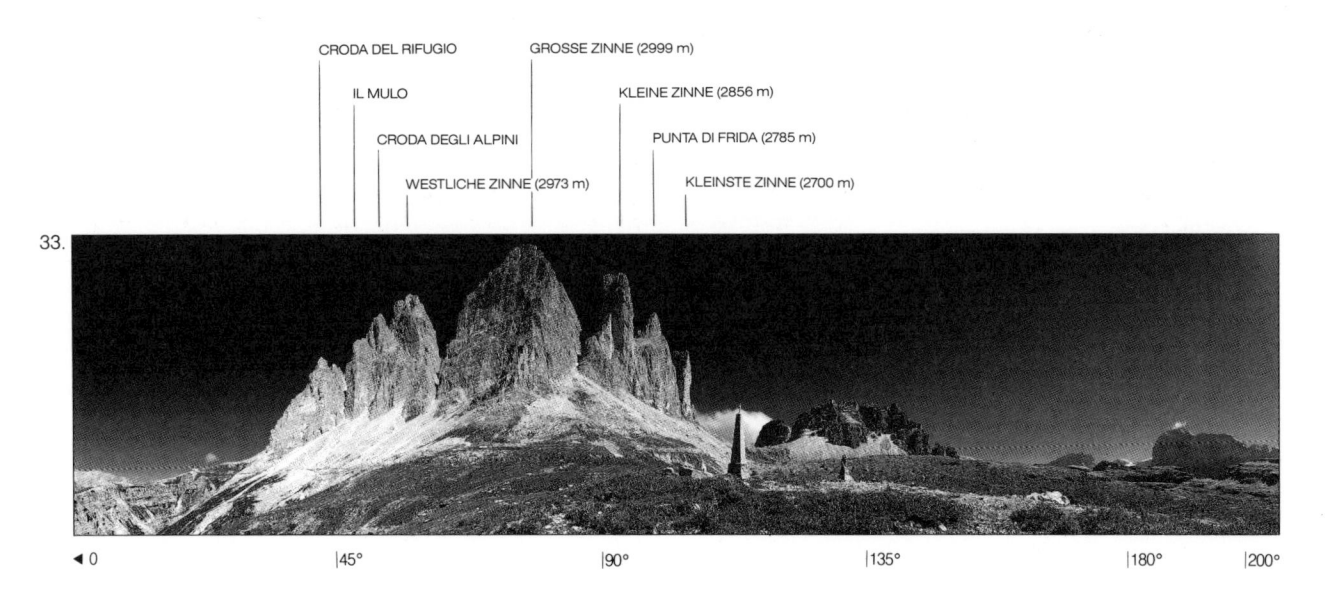

◀ 0 |45° |90° |135° |180° |200°

Die berühmten Nordwände der Drei Zinnen (Bild 32) sind ein Teil des Naturparks Sextener Dolomiten und eines der weltberühmten Wahrzeichen dieses Gebirges. Links eröffnet sich der Paternsattel. Die Erstbesteigung der Großen Zinne erfolgte im Sommer 1869 durch Paul Grohmann, Franz Innerkofler und Peter Salcher von Süden her. Die Kleine Zinne (2856 m) wurde im Juli 1881 von den Brüdern Michael und Hans Innerkofler besiegt, nachdem einige Tage vorher Ludwig Grünwald und der Führer Santo Siorpaes die nahe gelegene Punta di Frida (2805 m) erklommen hatten. Es mußten noch viele Jahre vergehen, ehe die furchteinflößenden Nordwände sich der Zähigkeit und technischen Gewandtheit der Bergsteiger beugten. Erst 1933 bezwang der Bergführer und legendäre Kletterer Emilio Comici in Begleitung von Angelo und Giuseppe Dimai aus Cortina die Nordwand der Großen Zinne. Von Süden aus (Bild 33) betrachtet, besitzen die Drei Zinnen zwischen Forcella Longères (mit der Schutzhütte Auronzo) und dem Paternsattel nicht die Stattlichkeit, die man von Norden her kennt; dennoch ist der Anblick beeindruckend. Von links sieht man die Croda del Rifugio, den Mulo, die Croda degli Alpini und die Westliche Zinne. Nach der Großen Zinnenscharte erheben sich die Große Zinne, darauf folgen die Kleine Zinnenscharte, die Kleine Zinne, Punta di Frida und die Kleinste Zinne.

The renowned North faces of the Three Peaks of Lavaredo stand within the Dolomiti di Sesto Nature Reserve and form one of the world's best-known emblems of the Dolomites. The Forcella di Lavaredo can be seen to the left of the group. It was Paul Grohmann yet again who was the first up the Cima Grande (2999 m), which he reached via the South face in the summer of 1869 along with Franz Innerkofler and Peter Salcher. The Cima Piccola (2856 m) fell to Michael Innerkofler and his brother Hans in July 1881 a few days after Ludwig Grünwald and the guide Santo Siorpaes had conquered the nearby Punta di Frida (2805 m). Many years were still to pass, however, before the daunting North faces surrendered to the doggedness and technical skills of another generation of climbers. It was not until 1933, in fact, that the legendary guide Emilio Comici, along with Angelo and Giuseppe Dimai of Cortina, got the better of the North face of the Cima Grande. The South side of the Three Peaks (No. 33) between Forcella Longères (with the Auronzo shelter) and Forcella Lavaredo lacks the impressive might of its fellow. It none the less strives to achieve a fine effect, aided and abetted by the vast screes that hem its base. From left to right, we can see the Croda del Rifugio, the Mulo, the Croda degli Alpini, and the Cima Ovest. The Forcella della Grande is followed, in the centre, by the Cima Grande, then the Forcella della Piccola, the Cima Piccola, the Punta di Frida, and the Cima Piccolissima.

MULAZ (2906 m)
CIMA DEI BURELONI (3130 m)
CIMA DELLA VEZZANA (3192 m)
CIMON DELLA PALA (3184 m)

34.

◀ 0 |45° |90° |135° |180° |200° |220° |240° |260° |280° |300° |320°

35.　36.　37.

Ein eindrucksvoller Blick von der Segantini-Hütte am Passo della Costazza (Bild 34) auf die Palagruppe (Pale di San Martino), die neben der Brenta wichtigste Gruppe der Trentiner Dolomiten. Sie wird von der Silhouette des Cimon inmitten der kühnen Nordkette beherrscht. Von links zeigen sich Monte Mulaz (2906 m), Cima dei Bureloni (3130 m) mit dem Campanile del Travignolo, Cima della Vezzana (3192 m), der Pravignolo-Paß und schließlich der bizarre Cimon della Pala (3184 m). Die außergewöhnlich schlanke Linie seines Nordwestgrats, vom Rolle-Paß aus betrachtet, gibt ihm den Beinamen »Matterhorn der Dolomiten«. 1869 versuchte derselbe Paul Grohmann, der mit den Führern Innerkofler und Salcher innerhalb weniger Wochen die Dreischusterspitze, den Langkofel und die höchste der Drei Zinnen erklommen hatte, vergebens die Besteigung des Cimon della Pala. E. R. Whitwell erreichte schließlich den Gipfel, indem er ihn am 2. Juni 1870 zusammen mit dem Schweizer Lavener und Santo Siorpaes aus Cortina von der Nordostseite anging. Eindrucksvolle Panoramen bereichern die Landschaft. Ein Beispiel dafür ist das Val Venegia (Bild 35), hier in einer im Winter entstandenen Aufnahme. Die Nordwände der Palagruppe stechen mit dem Campanile und der Cima di Valgrande, der Cima dei Bureloni, dem Campanile di Val Strut sowie der Cima della Vezzana hervor. Das Primiero liegt im östlichen Trentino und grenzt an die Provinz Belluno an. Das Tal konnte jahrhundertelang seine Tradition und ethnischen Charakteristika erhalten. Stille und eine romantische Atmosphäre stehen in deutlichem Kontrast zur wilden Berglandschaft. Deren monumentaler Kern bildet den Hintergrund für die Pfarrkirche von Transacqua (Bild 37), einer kleinen, durch die Palagruppe geschützten Ortschaft.

This engaging view (No. 34) from the Segantini Chalet at the Costanza Pass is of the Pale di San Martino, overlooked by the silhouette of the Cimón. This group stands within the rugged scenario of the Northern Chain and constitutes, along with that of the Brenta, the most substantial portion of the Trentino Dolomites. Starting from the left, we have the Mulaz (2906 m), the Cima dei Bureloni (3130 m) with the Campanile del Travignolo, the Cima della Vezzana (3192 m), the Travignolo Pass, and the Cimón della Pala (3184 m). The impressive upward sweep of its North-West spur, as seen from the Rolle Pass, explains its other title: »Matterhorn of the Dolomites«. Needless to say, the name of our Viennese acquaintance, Paul Grohmann, crops up once more. Accompanied by his guides, Innerkofler and Salcher, he collected the scalps of the Dreischusterspitze, the Langkofel and the Cima Grande di Lavaredo in the space of a few weeks in 1869. The Cimón della Pala sent him home empty-handed, however, in favour of E. R. Whitwell, who reached the top via the North-East face on 2 June 1870, together with the Swiss climber Lauener and Santo Siorpass, a guide from Cortina. The landscape hereabouts abounds in panoramas. An example is offered by Val Venegia, presented here in its winter clothing (No. 35) and dominated by the North faces of the Pale, with the Campanile and Cima di Valgrande, the Cima dei Bureloni, the Campanile di Val Strut, and the Cima della Vezzana. The Primiero lies in the Eastern part of the Trentino alongside the Province of Belluno. The valley has preserved its traditions and ethnic particularities. Serenity and a romantic atmosphere — in sharp contrast with the wild mountainscape — are the distinctive features of Pieve di Transacqua (No. 37), a small town under the lee of the Pale.

38.

Die bezaubernde Dolomitenlandschaft birgt eine sehr charakteristische und vielfältige Flora mit all ihrer typischen Anpassung an hohe Bergregionen. In einer Höhe von über 2000 Metern, an der Baumgrenze also, treffen wir auf ausgedehnte Bergwiesen, wo im Frühling und im Sommer lebhafte Farben aufblühen: das charakteristische Blau der Glockenblumen, das Violett des Bitterwurz, das Gelb der Primeln, das Hellrosa der Alpenglöckchen und nicht zuletzt die zarten Kuhschellen. An den Steilwänden finden die im Felsen lebenden Arten Unterschlupf; sie sind oft Relikte vergangener geologischer Epochen und müssen ihre Wurzeln tief in die Felsenritzen eingraben, um Wasser und Nahrung zu finden. Wir treffen hier auf die typischen Polster der Steinbrechgewächse und des Berg-Hahnenfußes, auf das berühmte Edelweiß und zahlreiche Fingerkrautgewächse, auf Sukkulenten wie die primula auricola und außerdem auf Flechten und Algen, die auf oder sogar direkt im Felsgestein wohnen. Selbst auf Geröllhalden wagen sich einige Blumen, z. B. der Bergmohn (papaverum alpinum), der Eis-Hahnenfuß, der bis zu einer Höhe von 4000 Metern anzutreffen ist, und der Almrausch (dryas octopedala). Wenn wir unter die 2000-Meter-Linie durch das Band von Latschenkiefern, Almrosen, Heidelbeeren und Wacholdern gehen, begegnen wir den ersten Bäumen: zuerst vereinzelte Lärchen, dann Mischwälder, die weiter unten den dichten Fichtenwäldern Platz machen, die bisweilen von Almen und fetten Weiden durchsetzt sind. Hier, zwischen den üppigen Gräsern, schauen weiße und rote Lilien hervor, Kohlröschen mit dem Duft der Vanille, gelbe Korbblütler, Disteln und der gelbe Enzian (gentiana lutea), der wegen der Heilkraft seiner Wurzeln wohlbekannt ist, und noch viele andere Blumen.

The splendid scenario of the Dolomites is not surprisingly the home of a varied flora displaying the usual forms of adaptation of plant life to the harsh environment of the highlands. Above the tree-line (2000 metres), we find extensive Alpine meadows, whose vivid colours are a joy in late spring and summer with their sky-blue campanulas, violet gentianellas, yellow primulas, purple pasque-flowers, and pale pink soldanellas. The steep faces offer protected microenvironments for saxatile species — often relicts — that strike their roots deep into the cracks in search of food and water. Examples include the pillowlike formations of saxifrages and androsaces, the engaging rock rampion, also known as the devil's claw from the shape of its flower, the well-known edelweiss, many cinquefoils, succulents, such as Primula auricola, and lichens and algae living on the surfaces or even inside the rocks. The slithering screes, too, offer a foothold for the yellow poppy (Papaverum alpinum), the ranunculus of the glaciers, which can even be found above 4000 metres, and extensive carpets of the Alpine rose (Dryas octopetala). Below the tree-line, of course, we meet a belt of scrub formed of rhododendrons, dwarf pines, myrtles, and junipers before the first trees appear: scattered larches, thickets with a variety of types, followed lower by thick fir woods, interspersed here and there with malgas and lush pastures, whose grasses are enlivened by white and red lilies, vanillascented mountain orchids (Nigritellae), yellow composites, thistles, the greater gentian (Gentiana lutea), whose root provides a tonic bitter, and many other flowers besides.

Panorama von der Punta Rocca (3309 m), dem Ostgipfel des Marmoladamassivs (Bild 39). Im Hintergrund erkennt man rechts Langkofel- und Sellagruppe. Im Herzen der Sextener Dolomiten (Bild 40) zeigt der Rundblick die zahlreichen Gipfel, die diesen herrlichen Teil der Alpen umschließen. Von links nach rechts: der Paßportenkopf in der kleinen Paterngruppe; über dem Fischleinpaß erhebt sich der zackige Elfer, der sich über den Zsigmondygrat fortsetzt, und der mächtige Zwölfer. In der Mitte die Parade der Marmarole, die Cadinspitzen, der Monte Cristallo, die Drei Zinnen und der breite Paternsattel. Hier scheint die Natur mehr als irgendwo sonst die einzigartige Vielfalt der dolomitischen Landschaft in einem einzigen Panorama vereint zu haben, das im Kontrast der Formen und Farben, im Licht- und Schattenspiel seine besondere Charakteristik findet.

A panorama of Punta Rocca (3309 m), the Eastern summit of the Marmolada massif. The Langkofel und Selle Groups can be seen in the right background. A 360° panorama in the heart of the Sesto Dolomites (No. 40) shows the many peaks crowning this superb segment of the Alps. From left to right: Croda del Passaporto in the tiny Paterno Group; beyond the Fiscalino Pass, the jagged Elfer, which continues with the Zsigmondy Ridge and the Zwölferkofel; in the centre, the Marmarole, the Cadini di Misurina, Monte Cristallo, the Tre Cime di Lavaredo, and the extensive Lavaredo Forcella. Here more than elsewhere Nature seems to have gathered together in a single »visual embrace« the incomparable variety of the Dolomite landscape, whose most distinctive feature is contrasting shapes and colours, and patches of light and shade.

42.

CIMA BRENTA ALTA (2960 m)
CIMA TOSA (3159 m)
CAMPANILE BASSO (2883 m)

43.

CIMA FALKNER (2999 m)
CIMA BRENTA (3150 m)
TORRE DI BRENTA (3014 m)
CAMPANILE ALTO (2937 m)
CROZZON DI BRENTA (3135 m)
CIMA TOSA (3159 m)

Die Brentagruppe in einer Ansicht von Madonna di Campiglio aus (Bild 41). Die Brentagruppe befindet sich im Westen der Provinz Trento (Trient) und breitet sich auf einer Länge von 45 Kilometern aus; im Norden wird sie vom Valle di Sole begrenzt und im Osten vom Nonstal. Die von Osten gemachte Winteraufnahme (Bild 42) zeigt von links nach rechts Brenta Alta (2960 m), Cima Tosa (3159 m), Campanile Basso (2883 m) und die Sfulmini. Die Brentagruppe wurde im Verhältnis zu den anderen Dolomitengruppen relativ spät entdeckt und erlebte ihre erste Erschließungswelle am Ende des letzten Jahrhunderts mit den Besteigungsversuchen am Campanile Basso, dem »phantastischen Felsobelisken«, der zwischen der Brenta Alta und dem Campanile Alto ungefähr 300 Meter in die Höhe ragt. Die Erstbesteigung gelang schließlich Otto Ampferer und Karl Berger am 18. August 1899. Seit dieser Zeit stellen die insgesamt 165 Gipfel der Brentagruppe ein ideales Kletterterrain dar, das Generationen von ehrgeizigen Bergsteigern herausgefordert hat. Die Ansicht des Hauptbereiches (Bild 43), aufgenommen bei Sonnenuntergang von Nordwesten gibt das Höhenprofil der Gipfel wieder (von links nach rechts): Grostèmassiv, Cima Falkner (2999 m) und Bocchetta del Tuckett; es folgen Cima Brenta (3150 m), Sfulmini mit dem Torre di Brenta (3014 m) und Campanilo Alto (2937 m); rechts von der Bocca die Brenta der Crozzon di Brenta (3135 m) und schließlich ganz rechts die Cima Tosa als höchster Gipfel der ganzen Gruppe.

The Brenta Dolomites seen from Madonna di Campiglio. On the right, the road leading to this tourist resort from Pinzolo. The group is located in the North-Western part of the Province of Trento and stretches for 45 km. It is bounded to the North by the Valle di Sole and the East by the Valle di Non. A winter view from the East side (No. 42) shows (from left to right) the peaks of Brenta Alta (2960 m), Cima Tosa (3159 m) and Campanile Basso (2883 m), and the Sfulmini Chain. The Brenta was brought into the Dolomite repertoire somewhat later than the other groups. Its mountaineering overture was played at the end of the 19th century, when the first attempts were made to reach the top of the Campanile Basso, »a fantastic obelisk« rising up for nearly three hundred metres between the Brenta Alta and the Campanile Alto. This was accomplished on 18 August 1899 by Otto Ampferer and Karl Berger. Since then, the 165 peaks of the Brenta Group have been an ideal training ground for generations of Alpinists. Our photo of the middle section (No. 43) was taken at sunset from the North-West shows several of the main peaks. Starting from the left: the Grostè Massif with Cima Falkner (2999 m) and the Bocchetta del Tuckett; Cime Brenta (3150 m), the Sfulmini Chain with Torre di Brenta (3014 m) and Campanile Alto (2937 m); Bocca di Brenta, Crozzón di Brenta (3135 m), and Cima Tosa (3159 m).

44.

45.

Das weite Talbecken, das sich nach Corvara im Gadertal hinabzieht, wird von der unverwechselbaren Silhouette (Bild 44) des Sass Songhér beherrscht. Auf der Linken der Sass da Ciampac und ganz links der Sellastock. Rechts die grüne Hochebene des Col Alto. Im Kontrast zwischen ausgedehnten Bergwiesen und den hervorstechenden Zinnen liegt der Reiz dieser Landschaft. Der Sass Songhér ist zu Recht das Wahrzeichen dieses ladinischen Tals, und er ist in den letzten Jahren immer mehr zu einem touristischen Ziel geworden. Unbekannte Jäger haben sich als erste auf den Gipfel des Sass Songhér gewagt; die Erstbesteigung über die Südwand erfolgte im August 1900 und wurde vom Österreicher Karl Berger zusammen mit den Talbewohnern Eduard Franzelin und Franz Kostner durchgeführt. Noch eine Ansicht des Gadertals (Bild 45) mit der langen Felsbastion des Heiligkreuzkofels (auf ladinisch Sass dla Crusc) über der Ortschaft Stern. Rechts von der Forcella Medesc erkennt man den Piz dla Varela und die Conturines.

The wide cirque sloping down towards Corvara in Val Badia is overshadowed by the unmistakable silhouette of the Sassongher, with the Sàss da Ciampac and the Sella Group on the left. and the green heights of the Col Alto on the right. Val Badia branches off from Val Pusteria and runs as fas as the slopes of its crown of massifs. A fine landscape is formed by this contrast between broad mountain pastures and beetling cliffs. The Sassongher itself (2665 m) is the very meet symbol of this Ladin valley, which has lately won the favour of tourists. Local hunters whose names have not been recorded were the first to set foot on the summit. The South face was conquered in August 1900 by the Austrian climber Karl Berger in the company of Eduard Franzelin and a guide, Franz Kostner. Another view of Val Badia (No. 45) with the long rampart of Heiligkreuzkofel (Ladin: Sàss dla Crusc) above the town of La Villa. The Piz dla Varela and the Piz dles Cunturines can be seen to the right of the Forcella Medesc.

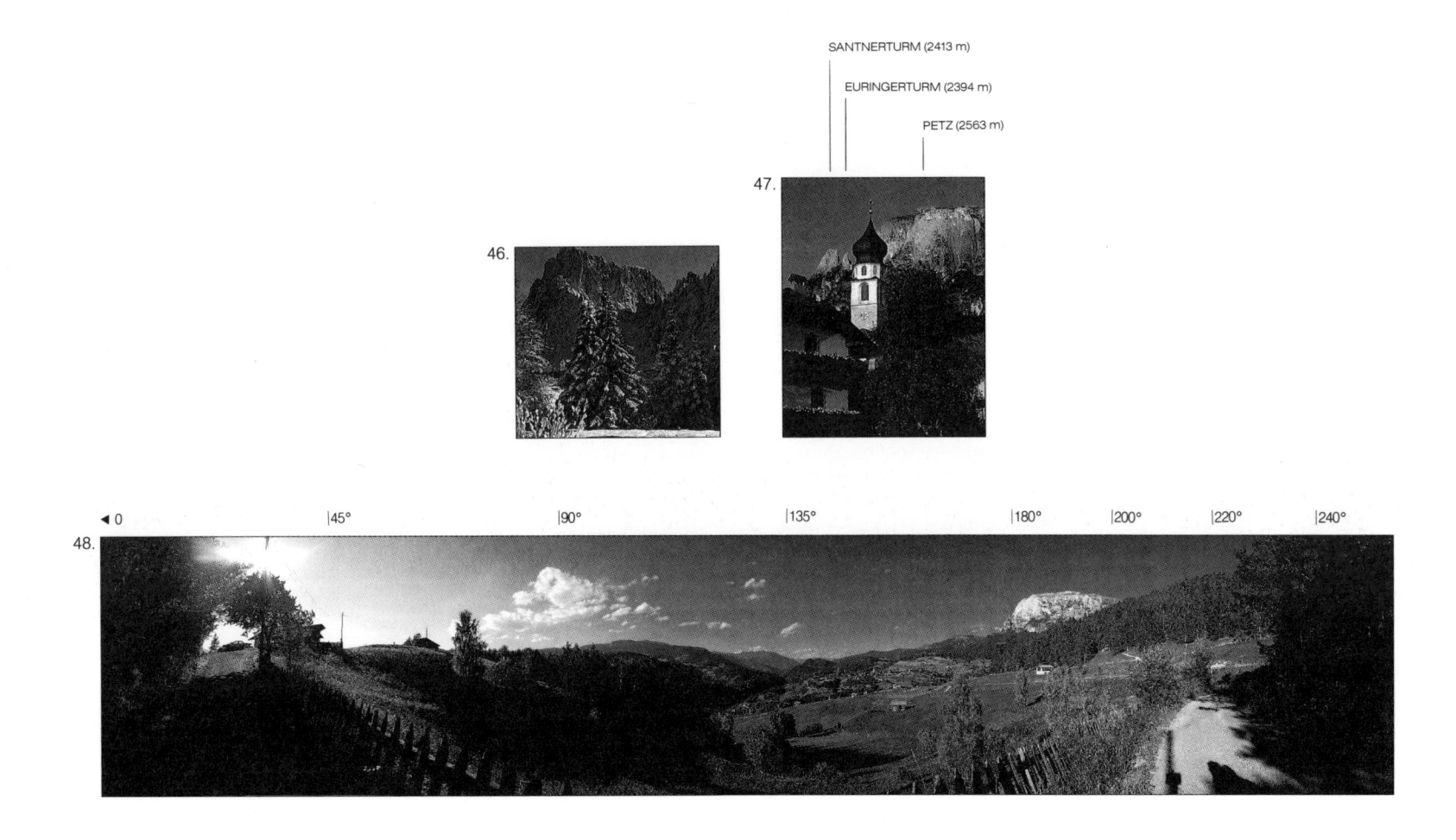

46.

47.

SANTNERTURM (2413 m)
EURINGERTURM (2394 m)
PETZ (2563 m)

48.

49.

50.

Eine winterliche Ansicht vom Langkofel, von der Seiser Alm aus aufgenommen (Bild 46). Der Langkofel, von vielen als »der schönste Dolomitenberg« bezeichnet, wird im Norden vom Fassatal, im Osten vom Grödnertal und im Westen von der Seiser Alm eingegrenzt, liegt also in den beiden Provinzen Bozen und Trento. Die Langkofelgruppe setzt sich aus fünf Hauptgipfeln zusammen: Langkofel (3181 m), Fünffingerspitze (2998 m), Grohmannspitze (3114 m), Zahnkofel (3000 m) und Plattkofel (2958 m). Den Gipfel des Langkofels bestieg 1869 Paul Grohmann zusammen mit den Führern Franz Innerkofler und Peter Salcher als erster. Hinter der Kirche von Völs am Schlern (Bild 47) erhebt sich das unverwechselbare Profil des Petz (2563 m) mit dem Santnerturm (2413 m) und dem Euringerturm (2394 m). Wir befinden uns im Schlern-Naturpark (Bild 48), der zwischen den Gemeinden Tiers, Völs und Kastelruth liegt und mit der Seiser Alm eine der meistgeschätzten und bekanntesten Regionen der Westlichen Dolomiten darstellt. Diese Hochebene liegt in einer durchschnittlichen Höhe von 1700 bis 2200 Metern. Die Alphörner der Männer von Marinzen (Bild 50) holen uns aus der versunkenen Betrachtung der Südtiroler Berge zurück. Tradition und Volkssitten lassen sich durch die immer bedrückender werdende »Fremdenverkehrsindustrie« nicht vertreiben; sie erhalten ihre vielfältigen Ausdrucksmöglichkeiten und bleiben wesentliche Kulturmerkmale der Bergbewohner.

The Langkofel (3181 m) seen from Alpe di Siusi. Classed by many as the most beautiful mountains in the Dolomites, the Langkofel Group is bounded to the North by Valle di Fassa, to the East by Val Gardena, and to the West by Alpe di Siusi. It thus lies in both the Province of Bolzano and the Province of Trento. It has five main peaks: Langkofel, Fünffingerspitze (2998 m), Grohmannspitze (3114 m), Zahnkofel (3000 m), and Plattkofel (2958 m). It was in 1869 that Paul Grohmann accompanied by two guides, Franz Innerkofler and Peter Salcher, made the first ascent of the Langkofel. The unmistakable outline of the Schlern (2563 m) with Punta Santner (2413 m) and Punta Euringer (2394 m) rises behind the church of Völs am Schlern (No. 47) in the Schlern Nature Reserve (No. 48), which lies in the municipalities of Tiers, Völs and Kastelruth and vies with Alpe di Siusi (No. 49) as one of the best-known and best-loved areas in the Western Dolomites. This tableland is from 1700 to 2200 metres in altitude. The traditional alpenhorns of the men of Marinzen (No. 50) complete for our attention with the breathtaking spectacle of the Alto Adige highlands. The ancient ways have not hung on as a sop to the ever-pressing claims of tourism, but persist in many forms of expression as an essential feature in the culture of the mountain folk.

51.

52.

Beeindruckende Winterlandschaft auf der Südseite des Sellajochs (Bild 51). Links des hochgelegenen Pordoipasses heben sich unverkennbar die Sellatürme ab. Der von ladinischen Talschaften umgebene Sellastock stellt einen der zentralen Punkte in den Dolomiten dar. Als ein Gebirge, das man nie ganz durchschaut, wurde es oft als beunruhigende und gar feindselige »Mondlandschaft« beschrieben, in der auch ein häufiger Gast immer wieder ungewohnte Einblicke, neue und abwechslungsreiche Eindrücke erhält. Der weite Blick vom Sellajoch aus (Bild 52) wird zur Linken von der Langkofelgruppe beherrscht. Am Horizont ganz hinten die Geislerspitzen und rechts die Sella mit dem schneebedecktem Piz Boè (3152 m), der höchsten Erhebung der ganzen Gruppe. Weiter rechts dann die Marmolada.

A fine winter landscape on the Alto Adige side of the Sella Pass. On the left of the Pordoi Pass further up, the Sella Towers. The Sella Group is surrounded by Ladin valleys. One of the fulcra of the whole of the Dolomites, its lunar landscape, often hostile and disquieting, has rendered it something of a terra incognita, and even its habitués expect to come away with new impressions, or discover unusual settings and scenarios for their delight. The Sella Pass (No. 52) is overlooked by the Langkofel Group on the left. The Odle Group can be made out on the distant horizon, while to the right we can locate the Sella with the snow-covered Piz Boé, the highest of these peaks (3152 m), and, still further to the right, the Marmolada.

PUNTA SERAUTA (2962 m)   PUNTA ROCCA (3309 m)   GRAN VERNEL (3210 m)
PIZ SERAUTA (3069 m)   PUNTA PENIA (3343 m)   RODA DEL MULON (2882 m)

53.

◀ 0 |45° |90° |135°

54.

Die Nordansicht der Marmolada (Bild 53), dem höchsten Berg der Dolomiten mit einer Gletscherfläche von mehr als drei Quadratkilometern. Die Gruppe erreicht in der Punta Penia (3343 m) ihren höchsten Punkt; dieser befindet sich rechts über dem Gletscher, und man erreicht ihn unter anderem auf dem Klettersteig über den Westgrat aus der Marmolada-Scharte (2896 m) direkt neben dem Piccolo Vernel. Rechts der Gran Vernel (3210 m) und die Roda del Mulon (2882 m), die gegen die Pian Trevisan hin abfallen, wo der Wildbach Avisio entspringt. Links erhebt sich eine aus dem Piz (3069 m) und der Punta Serauta (2962 m) gebildete gewaltige Barriere. Der mächtige Zauber, der von der Marmolada und ihren weiß schimmernden Schneefeldern ausgeht — ein Dorado für Bergsteiger und Kletterer — ist wohl nur noch mit dem der Drei Zinnen zu vergleichen. Sie wird »Königin der Dolomiten« genannt und auch oft als »vollkommener Berg« bezeichnet, vielleicht auch, weil man an ihren Hängen sowohl skilaufen als auch bergsteigen und klettern kann. Die Besteigungsversuche sind bis auf die ersten Jahre des letzten Jahrhunderts datierbar, als eine Gruppe von Talbewohnern erfolglos den waghalsigen Anstieg versuchte. Der höchste Gipfel, die Punta Penia, wurde jedoch erst Mitte des letzten Jahrhunderts bezwungen; 1864 wurde der legendäre Wiener Bergsteiger Paul Grohmann von den Führern Angelo und Fulgenzio Dimai aus Cortina auf den Gipfel begleitet.

The Northern slopes of the Marmolada, the highest peak in the Dolomites, covered with glaciers extending for more than three square kilometres. The group ends with Punta Penìa (3343 m), to the right of the glacier. This peak is reached along an aided route from the Forcella Marmolada (2896 m) near the Piccolo Vernel (3210 m), which can be seen on the right together with the Roda del Mulón (2882 m), two outposts that drop to Pian Trevisan, where the Avisio is born. On the left, there is the mighty barrier formed by the Piz (3069 m) and Punta Seràuta (2962 m). The fascination exerted by the Marmolada with its gleaming snowfields, the realm of Alpinists and climbers, is rivalled by that of the Three Peaks of Lavaredo alone. Dubbed the »queen« of the Dolomites, it is also referred to as the »perfect mountain«, one reason perhaps being that its slopes are suitable for winter sports as well as mountaineering. Attempts to climb these peaks were made without success by the people of the valley in the early years of the 19th century. It was not until 1864 that the ubiquitous Paul Grohmann, accompanied on this occasion by two guides from Cortina, Angelo and Fulgenzio, made the first ascent of the highest peak, Punte Penìa.

55.   56.

TORRE COLDAI (2600 m)
TORRE ALLEGHE (2649 m)
TORRE VALGRANDE (2715 m)
PUNTA CIVETTA (2920 m)
CIVETTA (3220 m)
PICCOLA CIVETTA (3207 m)
CIMA DE GASPERI (2994 m)
CIMA SU ALTO (2951 m)

57.

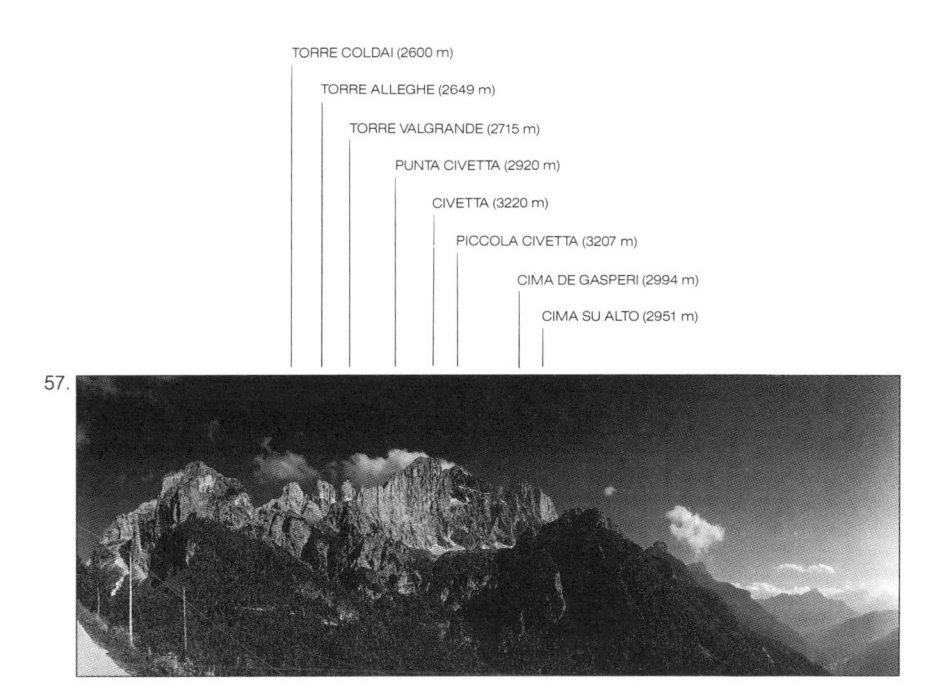

Die Nordwestwand der Civetta (3220 m) mit ihrem Hauptgipfel und der Piccola Civetta (Bild 55). In der Mitte sieht man das kleine, abschüssige Cristallo-Firnfeld. Links davon eröffneten 1926 Emil Solleder und Gustav Lettenbauer einen direkten Aufstieg, der als erster Kletteranstieg in den Dolomiten mit dem Schwierigkeitsgrad VI eingestuft wurde. Das Civettamassiv, das hinter der dunklen Silhouette des Col Rean (Bild 56) auftaucht, markiert den Mittelpunkt der Berggruppe, die sich in den Belluneser Dolomiten über dem See und der Ortschaft Alleghe erhebt. Mit ihrer »Wand der Wände« ist es sicherlich einer der faszinierendsten Bergstöcke des gesamten Alpenbogens; die stellenweise überhängende Wand, die fast 1200 Meter in die Höhe ragt, ist beeindruckend. Die folgende Aufnahme (Bild 57) zeigt von links nach rechts: Torre di Coldai (2600 m), Torre Alleghe (2649 m) und Torre Valgrande (2715 m), darauf folgen Torre da Lago (2713 m), Pan di Zucchero (2726 m) und Punta Civetta (2920 m). Rechts von den zwei höchsten Türmen, dem Civetta-Hauptgipfel und der Kleinen Civetta, erhebt sich der Knotenpunkt der Cime de Gasperi (2994 m) und des Su Alto (2951 m).

The North-West face of the Civetta (3220 m) and the two summits: the Civetta and the Piccola Civetta. In the centre, the Cristallo, a small hanging glacier, one of the few of this type in the Dolomites. It was to its left that Emil Sollender and Gustav Lettenbauer established a direct ascent, the first sixth-degree route in the Dolomites. It was among these faces, therefore, that modern climbing was born, and the leading experts of our century performed memorable feats. The Civetta Massif, emerging from the dark outlines of Col Reàn (No. 56), is the mid-point of the group of mountains soaring above the lake and town of Alleghe in the Belluno Dolomites. »The face par excellence«, as it has been rightly named, the Civetta is certainly one of the most fascinating in the Alps with its great wall rising sheer for nearly 1200 metres. The next photo (No. 57) shows the Coldài (2600 m), Alleghe (2649 m) and Valgrande (2715 m) Towers, followed by the Torre da Lago (2713 m), the Pan di Zucchero (2726 m) and Punta Civetta (2920 m). To the right of the highest peaks, the knot formed by Cima De Gasperi (2994 m) and Cima Su Alto (2951 m) are ready to test the climber's skill to the utmost.

58.

Cortina d'Ampezzo beschließt unsere Reise durch die Dolomiten mit der stolzen Gipfelkrone des Pomagagnón, der sich im Norden an den Monte Cristallo anschließt. Sie stellt für das Talbecken von Cortina eine natürliche Barriere dar, die es vor kalten Bergwinden schützt. Bei Sonnenuntergang wird sie zum Symbol aller Dolomitenberge. Die Worte von Karl Felix Wolff halten diesen magischen Augenblick fest: »Nun ist es Abend. Zwischen den Ästen der Lärchen erblicken wir die hohen Gipfel, die mit ihren kräftigen Farben leuchten. Rasch kehren wir zum Belvedere an der Ostseite der Crepa zurück. Cortina liegt schon im Schatten, einem Schatten mit bläulichem Glanz. Aber oben in der Höhe, über den Tälern, glühen jetzt die Dolomitenfelsen wie eine Art versteinerte Flamme am frostigen, grünlichen Himmel. Jeder dieser Berge hat seine eigene Farbe: Der Cristallo ist in Rot getaucht, der Sorapis in Gelb, der Antelao in ein Orangerot, das der Schnee sanft auflösen wird ... es ist der allerschönste und außergewöhnlichste Anblick.«

Our travels come to an end with Cortina d'Ampezzo crowned with the summits of the Pomagagnón, and linked to Monte Cristallo to the North. This natural barrier defending the Cortina valley from the icy Northern winds stands in the sun's dying rays as a symbol of the whole of the Dolomites. This is how Karl Felix Wolff captured such a magic moment: »Evening is upon us. Sublime peaks can be espied, resplendent in their glowing hues, between the boughs of larches. Another quick glance towards the Belvedere, on the Eastern side of the Crepa. Cortina is already bathed in shadows tinged with many shades of blue. Above, however, beyond the valleys, the ridges of the Dolomites are afire, petrified flames in the frozen greenish ether. Each mountain has its own tincture: the Cristallo gules, the Sorapis or, while the Antelào is clothed in a gently snowblanched orange surcoat ... the finest and the most marvellous of sights«.